MW00698898

OVERARCHING PRINCIPLES

1. Begin therapy with *clear goals*, and with "the end" in mind. Understand your clients *before* you expect to be understood by them. Accurate empathy and a strong therapeutic relationship are critically important to establish before you apply CBT techniques like cognitive restructuring. Don't jump in prematurely to fix problems before you fully understand the patient's world.

2. Take *global* problems or issues and focus on *specific* situations, emotions, and thoughts.

3. Emphasize teaching of an adaptable general method to deal with emotional problems rather than just solving the client's specific problem. Always ask what clients learned when they feel better.

4. *Track problems and symptoms over time.* Each session, use self-report questionnaires (i.e., Beck Depression or Anxiety Scales).

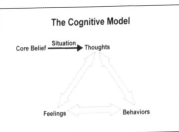

PSYCHOEDUCATION—THE CBT MODEL

- **Thinking and behavior are the focus of CBT.** Every moment of our existence can be broken into three components that interact: thinking (cognitions, automatic thoughts, and core beliefs), feeling (emotions and mood), and actions or behavior (including physiological reactions, such as an increased heart rate).

Rationale for CBT—Explain to your clients:

- Thoughts and behaviors are the focus of CBT, because these can change. We can indirectly control our feelings by changing our thinking and behavior.
- Automatic thoughts are a result of a client's underlying core beliefs related to themselves, the world, or the future.
- Symptoms of depression can be linked to thoughts and core beliefs that are activated by precipitating stressful life events.

DISCOVER: i. What is the patient's most important problem to work on *now*?
ii. What are the thoughts that interfere or get in the way of your client being able to problem solve?
iii. Why can't he handle the stressor that he is facing, the adversity in his life?
iv. How can I help my patient to see his situation and engage in behaviors that are more adaptive?

THE AUTOMATIC THOUGHT RECORD: FIRST THREE COLUMNS

6. **Use the Automatic Thought Record in all sessions, review, and assign as homework.** Look for patterns of core beliefs in the domains of lovability or achievement.

   1. Collaboratively focus on a specific situation in which a client experiences distress.

   2. Identify the emotions that she is experiencing in that situation.

3. Help her to identify and discover automatic thoughts, which are not always con-scious. Use the Downward Arrow Technique to identify core beliefs, asking her, "If a specific automatic thought were true, what it would mean to them?"

Questions to identify automatic thoughts can include the following:

"What was going through your mind just then?"

"What do you think you were thinking about just then, when you had this emotional shift?"

"What did this situation mean to you or mean about you or mean about the future?"

THE AUTOMATIC THOUGHT RECORD: LAST FOUR COLUMNS

7. *Socratic questioning, or guided discovery,* helps clients to change thinking and behaviors in combination with homework (see below). Teach clients to fill out thought records on their own in order to challenge their negative thoughts and generate alternative, more balanced thoughts.

COGNITIVE RESTRUCTURING STRATEGIES

- Operationalize the negative thought: a*sk for an example or definition* of a general-ized statement.
- *Evaluate the utility*, implications, advantages, and disadvantages (the impact) of the thought or the belief.
- *Look at the accuracy* of the belief (Columns #4 and #5 of the Automatic Thought Record).
- Look at their thoughts like ideas that may not be true by *classifying thoughts as pos-sible cognitive errors.*

David Burns's List of Cognitive Distortions

- All or nothing (black/white) - Labeling   - Jumping to conclusions
- Catastrophizing   - Magnification/minimization   - Overgeneralizing
- Disqualifying the positive   - Mental filter   - Should/must statements
- Emotional reasoning   - Mind reading

(It's not important to identify exact cognitive errors in specific situations because many could apply.)

- *Help clients to see alternative ways around the situation* by thinking to themselves in a more productive way. Ask, "*What would you say to a friend in the same situation?*" Invite them to align how they treat others to how they would treat themselves (Col-umn #6 of the thought record).
- Finally, have the clients *re-rate their moods* to see if there's any shift from the second column rating. An improvement will powerfully motivate clients to apply CBT on their own.

"Mark Fefergrad and Ari Zaretsky have written a concise, clear, and useful guide for those who want to learn the basics of cognitive behavioral therapy for depression. Filled with helpful forms and examples, this book is essential reading for those interested in the fundamentals of this treatment method. I highly recommend it!"

—**Robert L. Leahy, PhD**, Director,
American Institute for Cognitive Therapy;
Clinical Professor of Psychology,
Weill Cornell Medical College

Cognitive Behavioral Therapy for Depression

OTHER TITLES IN THE SERIES INCLUDE:

Cognitive Behavioral Therapy for Anxiety
Mark Fefergrad & Peggy Richter

Interpersonal Psychotherapy for Depression
Paula Ravitz, Priya Watson, & Sophie Grigoriadis

Motivational Interviewing for Concurrent Disorders
Wayne Skinner & Carolynne Cooper

Dialectical Behavior Therapy for Emotion Dysregulation
Shelley McMain & Carmen Wiebe

Achieving Psychotherapy Effectiveness
Molyn Leszcz, Clare Pain, Jon Hunter, Paula Ravitz, & Robert Maunder

A NORTON PROFESSIONAL BOOK

Cognitive Behavioral Therapy for Depression

Mark Fefergrad
Ari Zaretsky

SERIES EDITORS: Paula Ravitz and Robert Maunder

W. W. NORTON & COMPANY

New York | London

7-Column Thought Record used with permission; © 1983 Christine A. Padesky, PhD.
Copyright © 2013 by Mark Fefergrad, Ari Zaretsky, Paula Ravitz, and Robert Maunder

All rights reserved
Printed in the United States of America
First Edition

For information about permission to reproduce selections from this book, write to
Permissions, W. W. Norton & Company, Inc., 500 Fifth Avenue, New York, NY 10110

For information about special discounts for bulk purchases, please contact W. W. Norton
Special Sales at specialsales@wwnorton.com or 800-233-4830

Manufacturing by Quad Graphics
Book design by Kristina Kachele Design, llc
Production manager: Leeann Graham

Library of Congress Cataloging-in-Publication Data
Fefergrad, Mark.
Cognitive behavioral therapy for depression / Mark Fefergrad, Ari Zaretsky. — First edition.
pages cm. — (Psychotherapy essentials to go)
"A Norton professional book."
Includes bibliographical references.
ISBN 978-0-393-70828-8 (pbk.)
1. Depression, Mental—Treatment—Handbooks, manuals, etc. 2. Cognitive therapy—
Handbooks, manuals, etc. I. Zaretsky, Ari. II. Title.
RC537.F44 2013
616.85'270651—dc23
                2013008180

ISBN: 978-0-393-70828-8 (pbk.)

W. W. Norton & Company, Inc., 500 Fifth Avenue, New York, N.Y. 10110
www.wwnorton.com
W. W. Norton & Company Ltd., Castle House, 75/76 Wells Street, London W1T 3QT

1 2 3 4 5 6 7 8 9 0

Mark Fefergrad

Thank you very much to all my patients and teachers who
have educated me over the years. Even greater thanks to
my wonderful, beautiful, devoted, and caring wife, whose
support and love have been without boundary.

Ari Zaretsky

Dedicated to Mona, Lauren, Alex, and Daniel.

Mark Fefergrad, MD, MEd, is Assistant Professor and the Director of Postgraduate Education in the Department of Psychiatry at the University of Toronto. He has held several leadership roles with respect to CBT education and is the head of Cognitive Behavioral Therapy at Sunnybrook Health Sciences Centre.

Ari Zaretsky, MD, Associate Professor in the Department of Psychiatry at the University of Toronto and Psychiatrist-in-Chief at Sunnybrook Health Sciences Centre, has extensive experience in CBT treatment, teaching, and supervision.

Paula Ravitz, MD, is Associate Professor, Morgan Firestone Psychotherapy Chair, and Associate Director of the Psychotherapy, Health Humanities, and Education Scholarship Division for the Department of Psychiatry at the University of Toronto, where she leads IPT training. She is also the director of the Mt. Sinai Psychotherapy Institute. Her clinical practice, teaching, and research focus on IPT and attachment-informed psychotherapy.

Robert Maunder, MD, is Associate Professor in the Department of Psychiatry at the University of Toronto and head of research for Mount Sinai Hospital's Department of Psychiatry. His primary research interest is the role of interpersonal attachment on health.

Contents

Acknowledgments ix

Series Introduction xi

1 Introduction to Cognitive Behavioral Therapy for Depression 1

2 Learning Objectives 13

3 Fundamentals of CBT for Depression 15

4 The Automatic Thought Record and Socratic Questioning 21

5 Cognitive Restructuring 27

6 CBT Homework and Behavioral Therapeutic Strategies 33

7 Concluding Remarks 39

Lesson Plans 41

Quiz 51

APPENDIX A: Role-Play Transcripts 61

APPENDIX B: Practice Reminder Summary 83

APPENDIX C: Answer Key 89

References 99

Acknowledgments

Producing *Psychotherapy Essentials to Go* has depended on and benefited from the support and expertise of many people. We wish to acknowledge and thank Aaron T. Beck and Christine Padesky, the developers of Cognitive Behavioral Therapy, who, with others, have built the foundation from which this treatment has grown. We are grateful to the contributing authors whose hard work, wisdom, and creativity as educators and clinicians are represented; the Ontario Ministry of Health and Long Term Care, who provided funding to the educational outreach pilot project team of the Northern Psychiatric Outreach Program at the Centre for Addiction and Mental Health (CAMH); Nancy McNaughton and the University of Toronto Standardized Patient Program; Robert Swenson and the Ontario Psychiatric Outreach Program; the University of Toronto Department of Psychiatry; the Mount Sinai Hospital Department of Psychiatry; Molyn Leszcz and the Morgan Firestone Psychotherapy Chair; Scott Mitchell; the Canadian Mental Health Association's Northern Ontario branch executive directors and healthcare workers; and Andrea Costella Dawson and Sophie Hagen of W. W. Norton. We also wish to thank Robert Cooke, the CAMH, the actors who brought the material to life, Tom and Reet Mae and Ryan Hannabee of Mae Studios, Bhadra Lokuge, Connie Kim, and Lynn Fisher.

Series Introduction

Psychotherapy works. Meta-analyses demonstrate that psychotherapy reduces the symptoms and impact of the mental disorders that most commonly interfere with people's lives, including depression, anxiety, and the extraordinary challenges that emerge from concurrent addictions, mental illnesses, and personality disorders. The consensus treatment guidelines that provide clinicians with evidence-based direction for treating depression, anxiety, and other mental disorders recommend psychotherapy, sometimes as a first line of treatment.

At the same time, practicing *effective* psychotherapy is very challenging. For one thing, treatment guidelines recommend specific modalities of psychotherapy for specific disorders, such as Interpersonal Psychotherapy (IPT) for depression, Cognitive Behavioral Therapy (CBT) for depression or anxiety, Motivational Interviewing (MI) for mental health issues and substance abuse disorders, and Dialectical Behavior Therapy (DBT) for borderline personality disorder. Therapists working at the front lines of mental healthcare see *all* of these problems, but acquiring extensive supervision, training, and certification in any one of these modalities is costly and challenging, and being an expert in all types of psychotherapy is virtually impossible. How can a front-line therapist use the core skills of different modalities of psychotherapy effectively to help his or her clients overcome the debilitating effects of mental illness?

Psychotherapy Essentials to Go responds to the challenge that therapists who are not (yet) experts face in acquiring the core skills of psychotherapy. It is designed to be useful for both new therapists and those who are more experienced but want to learn the core techniques of different types of psychotherapy. It also is a refresher course on the techniques that experienced therapists are already familiar with.

This project emerged in response to the needs of mental healthcare workers who were facing extraordinary challenges. Working in community clinics in remote, underserviced areas, these clinicians were unable to provide psychotherapy to their clients because they had minimal psychotherapy training and limited means of acquiring it. Caseloads were often heavy and resources for referring clients to psychotherapists were extremely limited. These clinicians wanted but were unable to use psychotherapeutic techniques to help their clients suffering from depression, anxiety, and concurrent disorders. Needless to say, it was not feasible for these health workers to obtain the training, observation, and close supervision that are required to become experts in specific modalities of psychotherapy. Surely, there was a better alternative than providing no psychotherapy at all!

Drawing on the wealth of expertise of the contributing authors in this series, who are all faculty or staff at teaching hospitals affiliated with the University of Toronto, we created the videos that are at the core of the *Psychotherapy Essentials to Go* materials, as well as all of the accompanying lesson plans in order to meet the needs of clinicians and their clients. The materials worked. We tested the materials that we developed with healthcare workers of several disciplines and levels of experience including the caseworkers in community mental healthcare clinics whose needs initiated the project, medical students, nurses, family medicine and psychiatry residents, and social workers. Their knowledge increased, they used the techniques they had learned, and they reported that they had become more confident and effective clinicians, even with difficult clients. Even seasoned therapists benefited from brushing up on the specific therapy protocols (Ravitz et al., 2013).

The first five books and DVDs of the *Psychotherapy Essentials to Go* series teach the skills of Motivational Interviewing, Cognitive Behavioral Therapy (for anxiety and for depression), Dialectical Behavior Therapy, and Interpersonal Psychotherapy. These materials are not intended to replace full training in these evidence-supported psychotherapies; rather, they introduce and demonstrate techniques that clinicians and students can integrate into their care of people with common mental health problems.

The sixth book and its accompanying DVD address psychotherapy effectiveness across every modality of therapy. Regardless of which type of psychotherapy a therapist provides, doing psychotherapy requires therapists to be flexible and responsive to their clients. Also therapists and clients must form and sustain a strong working relationship: the therapeutic alliance. In every modality of psychotherapy, a good thera-peutic alliance leads to better clinical outcomes. With some clients the challenges encountered in forming and maintaining an alliance provide a window into the interpersonal difficulties that the clients experience in their other important relationships. This final book on psychotherapy effectiveness synthesizes the most important common factors of psycho-therapies and provides a therapist with an approach to understanding and managing challenges to establishing and maintaining a therapeutic alliance.

Learning psychotherapy means *changing how you behave* as a clin-ician—and changing habitual behavior is notoriously difficult. Learning new professional behavior takes time and practice—you need to *experi-ence* a new way of behaving. It isn't enough to read about it or hear about it. Experiential learning is most effective when it includes demonstration, modeling, and practice. For each book in the series, we suggest that you first watch the DVD, then read the accompanying text, and then follow the instructions in the lesson plans to practice and consolidate your learning. Take the quiz before starting this process in order to assess your baseline knowledge, and then take it again after having completed all four of the lessons, in order to assess your progress. Afterward, use the summary card of practice reminders in your daily clinical work.

For those interested in more training, further reading and clinical supervision are recommended. We hope that the techniques presented in these introductory *Psychotherapy Essentials to Go* materials will expand your clinical repertoire and will improve your competence and confi-dence in working with clients with mental health problems.

A couple of notes about language. First, those who provide care and treatment for people with mental health problems, and individuals who receive that care, prefer a wide range of names for those roles, and some have strong feelings about their preferences. For the sake of consistency, throughout this series we refer to the former individuals as "therapists" (occasionally opting for "clinicians" for the sake of some variety of expression) and the latter as "clients." We do this in spite of the fact that some modalities of psychotherapy are explicit about which terms are preferable (for example, IPT manuals refer to the person receiving the therapy as a patient, in keeping with the centrality of the medical model in IPT). We hope these are read to be the inclusive and nonprescriptive choices that are intended. Second, although pronouns in English are gendered, the gender of the therapists and clients we are discussing is usually irrelevant. We have opted for the phrases "he or she" and "his or her" except for a few passages where pronouns were required so frequently that it became too awkward. In those sections we have settled on one gender indiscriminately, with the intention that the "hes" and "shes" will balance out in the end.

Paula Ravitz and Bob Maunder

Introduction to Cognitive Behavioral Therapy for Depression

Cognitive Behavioral Therapy (CBT) is an evidence-based, first-line intervention for the treatment of depression and other illnesses. It has become one of the most researched modalities in the treatment of mental illness, with demonstrated efficacy for a wide range of clinical difficulties (Beck, Rush, Shaw, & Emery, 1979). In this introduction, we review some of the substantial and growing evidence for the use of CBT in the treatment of major depressive disorder. We will also illustrate the basic cognitive model, therapeutic stance, and some of the most important cognitive and behavioral interventions. When used with the accompanying video, clinical demonstrations, and learning guide, we hope that learners of all levels will be able to learn basic CBT principles and skills or enhance their prior knowledge and skills. A word of caution: We appreciate that this book is intended for a broad range of helping professionals. This means that it will not be sophisticated enough to deal with every individual challenge or presenting complaint that you might encounter in the real world. In our view, clinical supervision is a necessary component to ultimately becoming an independent, competent, and effective therapist.

COMMON FACTORS

In addition to the specific techniques of CBT, such as the Automatic Thought Record, it is important to recognize that "common factors" are extremely important to therapeutic outcomes. These are the beneficial characteristics that are common to all modalities of psychotherapy. Common factors are generally related to elements of the therapeutic relationship. Any successful therapy is grounded in an open, strong, genuine therapeutic relationship, which Carl Rogers called the "helping relationship." Without being skilled in forming and maintaining this relationship, no therapist is likely to use specific techniques and be effective. One can think of the specific techniques related to any therapeutic modality as the parts of an automobile. In that analogy, the common factors would be represented by the gasoline (i.e., the stuff that makes the car go).

Rogers defines a helping relationship as "a relationship in which one of the participants intends that there should come about, in one or both parties, more appreciation of, more expression of, more functional use of the latent inner resources of the individual" (1961). There are three characteristics that Rogers (1957) states are essential and sufficient for therapeutic change as well as being vital aspects of the therapeutic relationship:

1. The therapist's genuineness within the helping relationship. The therapist must "freely and deeply" be him- or herself. The therapist needs to be a real human being, not an omniscient, all-powerful, rigid, or controlling figure.
2. The therapist should have unconditional positive regard. This aspect of the helping relationship involves experiencing a warm acceptance of each aspect of clients' experience. There are no conditions put on accepting and caring for clients as who they are.
3. The therapist should have accurate empathy. An accurate understanding of the client's awareness of his or her own experience is crucial. It is essential to have the ability to enter the client's "private world" and understand his or her thoughts and feelings without judgment.

A review conducted by Lambert and Barley (2001) summarized over 100 studies concerning the therapeutic relationship and psychotherapy outcome. They focused on four areas that influenced the client's outcome: extra-therapeutic factors, expectancy effects, specific therapy techniques, and common factors/therapeutic relationship factors. Within these 100 studies, they calculated the contribution of each predictor to the outcome. Forty percent of the outcome was due to factors outside the therapy, 15% to expectancy effects, 15% to specific therapy techniques, and 30% to the therapeutic relationship or common factors. Lambert and Barley concluded that "Improvement in psychotherapy may best be accomplished by learning to improve one's ability to relate to clients and tailoring that relationship to individual clients" (p. 357).

CBT THERAPIST STANCE

Certain basic principles of the therapist's orientation to the client are specific to Cognitive Behavioral Therapy. First, the therapeutic focus is generally on the "here and now," rather than on the early experiences that contribute to core beliefs. The CBT therapist works collaboratively, engaging with the client to enable the mutual discovery of a more realistic or adaptive perspective. The core techniques used to achieve this result in CBT are Socratic questioning and the gathering of empiric evidence.

Socratic questioning promotes mutual discovery. This involves asking questions that are designed to better understand the client's difficulties without judgment. For example, a therapist working with a client who wishes to be more socially engaged would, instead of giving advice, ask about a specific behavioral task and potential obstacles she may encounter or about her beliefs and fears about this activity.

Socratic questioning facilitates gathering empirical evidence, which refers to collecting information about the client's experiences in order to help disconfirm (or sometimes support) depressogenic beliefs. One technique that assists with gathering evidence is the Automatic Thought Record, which allows clients to form their own more balanced conclusions regarding their beliefs.

THE STRUCTURE OF CBT

Because CBT is a short-term intervention, some structure to the overall therapy and the individual sessions helps to maintain focus on the most relevant issues. Psychoeducation about the nature of the client's illness

and symptoms, which serves to normalize her experience, is an important early step. Psychoeducation should include relevant information
regarding depression and a range of treatment options, including drug
treatment alternatives when relevant. "Socialization to the model" is
often used to describe the treatment parameters, framework, and the im-
portance of therapeutic tasks in CBT. As with most short-term therapies,
clients are engaged in setting specific, measurable, and achievable goals
for the course of treatment. Typical goals might include the ability to
return to work, greater functional capacity, or symptom relief.

Following an agreement on goals, the middle phase of treatment
generally focuses on acquiring skills and implementing more adaptive behaviors. These efforts are consolidated through the use of collaboratively
assigned homework between sessions. Homework is an essential component of CBT, serving to reinforce the mastery of skills and to provide
opportunities to challenge long-held dysfunctional beliefs. Homework
also serves as an important marker of adherence, motivation, and progress, and it provides a tool to identify real-life obstacles that may interfere
with the client's success after termination.

Each individual session generally follows a structured approach.
Typical elements include an update of important events since the last
session, a check on core mood and depressive symptoms, the setting of
a collaborative agenda, a review of homework (including problem solving
if needed), and the establishment of new homework tasks. Checking in
on the therapeutic relationship and the client's sense of alliance with the
therapist are also important. In preparing for termination, it is desirable
for your client to discuss his thoughts and feelings about the end of ther-

apy and to identify supports and techniques that will help him moving forward. Additionally, one would typically discuss relapse recognition and prevention.

THE COGNITIVE MODEL OF DEPRESSION

The fundamentals of contemporary cognitive theory were developed by Aaron T. Beck in the latter half of the twentieth century. Beck, who was originally trained as a psychoanalyst, became interested in the unconscious content of the dreams of depressed persons. Rather than uncovering repressed rage, as psychoanalytic theory predicted, his clients dreamed about situations in which they were incompetent or ineffective (Beck & Hurvich, 1959).

This led Beck to develop a new cognitive model of depression. Specifically, he saw strong links among affective states, cognitions, and behaviors, and he recognized that this provided an opening for a new therapeutic paradigm. Beck's CBT approach to depression was then expanded to anxiety and other mental health problems, such that cognitive therapy became the most empirically validated treatment modality (Beck et al., 1979), particularly for mood and anxiety disorders. CBT has since been incorporated into numerous consensus treatment guidelines around the globe (Beck, 2005).

The basic cognitive model posits that thoughts and behaviors are related to emotional states. Because people cannot control their emotions directly, the two main points of therapeutic intervention lie in the cognitive and behavioral realms. This is true for the treatment of all psychiatric disorders with CBT.

The cognitive triad consists of three major cognitive patterns that contribute to depression. First, clients with depression tend to have a negative view of themselves, and they tend to attribute unpleasant experiences to personal defects. The client believes that because of presumed defects, he or she is undesirable or worthless. Second, clients with depression tend to think negatively about the world or others. Beck says, "He sees the world as making exorbitant demands on him and/ or presenting insuperable obstacles to reaching his life goals. He mis-interprets his interactions with his animate or inanimate environment as representing defeat or deprivation" (1979, p. 11). Third, clients have negative views about the future. "As the depressed person makes long-range projections, he anticipates that his current difficulties or suffering will continue indefinitely. He expects unremitting hardship, frustration and deprivation. When he considers undertaking a specific task in the immediate future, he expects to fail" (Beck et al., 1979, p. 11).

There are also certain behaviors that are classically associated with depression. Clients tend to be anhedonic and enervated. They will often avoid interactions with others. Depending on the intensity of their symp-toms, they may remain at home or in bed for extended periods of time. In the most severe cases, clients with depression will contemplate or act on suicidal wishes. In the context of the cognitive model, all of these behaviors "make sense." If one thinks negatively about oneself, others, and the world, it follows that one would be disinterested in attempting novel tasks, engaging with others, or even enduring any misery. As such, it is the task of treatment to help correct some of the clients' cognitive misperceptions and to encourage more adaptive modes of behavior in order to facilitate an improved emotional state.

COGNITIVE INTERVENTIONS

Cognitive interventions are intended to help modify extreme or inaccurate depressive thoughts in an attempt to make them more balanced. This process has the potential to help a client view her situation more realistically. Because thoughts, emotions, and behaviors all link to each other in the cognitive model, this may also help her to feel better and behave in a more adaptive fashion. There are many different cognitive techniques. The following paragraphs will highlight only a few of the most important.

The Automatic Thought Record is a seven-column tool that helps clients to identify thoughts and feelings in specific triggering situations. These thoughts are called "automatic thoughts" because they occur spontaneously, are situationally dependent, and are generally accepted as valid without questioning. Although some clients will readily identify these thoughts, others need Socratic questioning or the use of the Downward Arrow Technique (shown in the video) in order to recognize them. The thought record then goes on to elaborate the evidence that supports or goes against the client's initial anxious thoughts. The sixth column allows for the development of a "balanced thought," reflecting a more accurate view of the situation than the client's initial biased perceptions. The final column asks the client to rate her mood states so as to concretize the emotional impact of this new balanced way of thinking. This entire process helps a client go from a view of the world that is heavily influenced by depressive thinking and early experiences to one that is more objective and realistic, given the situation in front of her. Similarly, a CBT therapist may ask a client to imagine "what she would say to a friend." This technique has a similar function of helping a client to distance herself from her dysfunctional thinking and adopt a more adaptive response.

The above techniques rely on a rational approach, meaning that they try to clarify the validity of a given thought. However, several interventions rely on a more constructivist viewpoint. This philosophy suggests that the accuracy of a thought is less important than the impact of it. These tools tend to be most useful where the accuracy of a thought cannot be known with certainty (e.g., when another person's motivation is in question) or when there is an issue of motivation on the part of the client. One simple way of looking at the utility of a given thought is to have the client make a simple list of the advantages and disadvantages of a particular way of thinking or behaving. In the case where someone else's motives are uncertain, one might look at the advantages and disadvantages of assuming that the other person is acting with malice. Alternatively, in an attempt to encourage a healthy behavior such as exercise, a client may make a list of the "pros" and "cons" of working out. Generally, at the moment that a decision must be made, the "cons" tend to be much more salient. This sort of technique allows clients to be more conscious of the "pros," which often involve longer-term thinking.

BEHAVIORAL INTERVENTIONS

Disrupting clients' depressive behavioral patterns is extremely important for several reasons. First, in the cognitive model, behaviors represent a major area in which a client can directly effect change. Furthermore, clients with moderate or severe depression often find it difficult to engage in cognitive exercises because of the effects of depression on their energy, concentration, and motivation. In addition, when depressed clients lie in bed alone, they are often left to ponder their depressive thoughts. They may think "I'm such a loser" or "I used to be so much more functional than this" or "Nobody cares about me; I'm all alone." In the absence of CBT techniques or distraction (and remembering the link between thoughts and feelings), these kinds of activities and their associated thoughts almost always worsen depressive symptoms. Finally, behavioral interventions, when properly instituted, hold the potential to have rapid and sometimes immediate impacts on function and learning.

One common behavioral intervention is known as activity monitoring. In collaboration with the therapist, the client is given a blank schedule that accounts for each hour of the day throughout the week. Clients are then asked to fill in each box with any activity in which they engaged during that hour. In addition, they are asked to rate each activity from 0 to 100 on scales of "pleasure" and "mastery." The pleasure rating is fairly self-explanatory and relates to the joy a client experiences while engaging in the given activity. Mastery refers to a sense of accomplishment. For example, most people do not find cleaning the dishes to be a particularly pleasurable activity, but having a cleaner home may result in a sense of mastery over one's surroundings. Similarly, eating an ice-cream cone generally does not lead to a sense of mastery, but most people will find it pleasurable. The purpose of this intervention is two-fold. First, in completing this chart over the course of a week, clients will begin to recognize that their depression is not monolithic. In fact even in the most severe depression, clients will report some fluctuation in their mood over the course of the day. This is important because the task then becomes to increase the amplitude, frequency, and duration of the mood fluctuations, which takes the client away from the "black or white" thinking associated with an unchanging mood state. In addition, reviewing the document can help to identify the activities most associated with positive moods and the activities that are most depressogenic. This is useful information for behavioral activation.

Behavioral activation involves asking clients to engage in particular activities. This follows from the fact that depressed clients who do nothing will be left with their depressive thoughts and will continue to view themselves as inadequate and ineffective. Some of these activities may be informed by the activity monitoring above. Other actions may be prescribed on the basis of likely mood-elevating activities such as exercise or social interaction. Clients are encouraged to engage in these behaviors without specific expectations. They are, however, asked to monitor and rate their mood (often before, during, and after the activity). This information can then be used to plan the next round of behavioral interventions.

One other behavioral intervention relates to what is known as the "behavioral experiment." As in other components of treatment with CBT, there is no expected or desired outcome. Rather, a client will engage in a collaboratively designed experiment in order to test a belief. For example, a depressed client may claim that he cannot call a friend because he has been out of touch for 3 months as a result of his depressive symptoms. In that instance, he may predict a negative reaction from the friend. Planning with the therapist is required so as to minimize the interference of potential obstacles. He is then encouraged to call the friend to see if the prediction matched the outcome. Because the thinking of depressed clients is often distorted, their predictions are frequently proven to be false. This experiential disconfirmation can then be used as leverage in the service of balancing depressive thoughts or engaging in additional behavioral experiments.

CONCLUSION

Although accurate empathy and emotional attunement are necessary preconditions for effective CBT treatment, they are not sufficient. CBT provides therapists with a coherent, empirically supported model of psychopathology and a methodology to help clients feel better and cope more effectively by teaching them essential skills to become their own therapists. Both the client and the therapist are expected to be highly active in CBT, and the therapist aims to deploy both cognitive and behavioral techniques to promote immediate and durable change. Cognitive techniques focus initially on using specific tools like the Automatic Thought Record to help clients recognize the link between their thoughts and their emotional reactions. After this specific skill has been mastered, the therapist teaches the client various cognitive restructuring techniques in order to cope more adaptively with stressful situations. Behavioral techniques can initially be used independently of cognitive restructuring techniques, and this approach should be utilized if the client is particularly depressed, hopeless, and inactive. Ideally, however, behavioral techniques such as activation, activity scheduling, and problem solving should be linked to cognitive techniques so that these become behavioral experiments that ultimately challenge the clients' underlying negative assumptions and beliefs about themselves and the world.

2 :: Learning Objectives

The objective of this book and DVD on Cognitive Behavioral Therapy for Depression is to help you acquire clinical skills using CBT. For those of you who have some experience with CBT, we hope that you will consolidate what you have already learned and will acquire some new techniques of therapeutic communication to integrate into your clinical practice.

At the end of this book, we hope that you will be able to achieve these goals:

1. Describe the cognitive model and the cognitive formulation for depression.
2. Utilize focused interviewing techniques to identify critical thoughts that are related to your clients' problems.

3. Utilize Socratic questioning to promote guided discovery for cognitive restructuring.

4. Apply five distinct cognitive restructuring techniques that promote change.

5. Implement behavioral activation techniques in order to improve a client's depressed mood.

Mark Fefergrad and Ari Zaretsky

3 :: Fundamentals of CBT for Depression

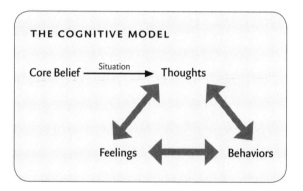

THE COGNITIVE MODEL

Core Belief ——Situation——▶ Thoughts

Feelings ◀——————▶ Behaviors

The idea of the cognitive model goes back to the Greek Stoic philoso-
phers. Epictetus stated that "it is not events that disturb people, it is their
judgments concerning them" (Epictetus, 2008, p. 222). Cognitive Behavioral Therapy focuses on changing the views that people take of things.

Aaron T. Beck, the founder of CBT, applied this understanding
of human nature to the formulation of a psychotherapy that focuses
on people's thinking. When thoughts are made explicit, they can be
challenged.

We can divide every moment of our existence into three components
of thoughts, feelings, and behaviors: what we are thinking, what we are
feeling, and what we are doing. Behavior includes what is happening

overtly and what is occurring inside our body. Physiological reactions, such as an increased heart rate, are included in the CBT definition of behavior.

What one thinks, what one does, and what one feels are all connected. It doesn't matter what comes first; they all *interact*.

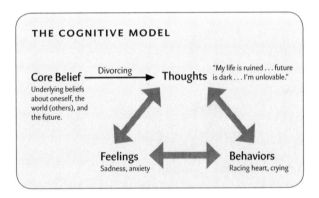

For example, a client who is going through a divorce may experience intense emotions of sadness and anxiety. She may feel these emotions in her body by having an increased heart rate. You might see her crying, and she might have some specific thoughts that are identifiable if you ask about them. She might be thinking to herself, "My life is ruined . . . the future is dark for me" or "I'm unlovable." These are the kinds of thoughts, or cognitions, that might be going through someone's mind in such a situation. Thoughts, feelings, and behaviors are linked to one another.

When providing your clients with a rationale for CBT, you will need to explain that this model focuses on thoughts and behaviors. Thoughts and behaviors are within their power to change. Clients have some control over their cognitions and behaviors, but they have less direct control over their feelings. However, feelings can be altered by shifting cognitions and behaviors.

Where do particular thoughts come from in a specific situation? Why does your client react the way she does in that specific situation? People have automatic thoughts because they have underlying core beliefs. These are implicit, perhaps unconscious beliefs. Depressive core beliefs are usually related to self, to others, and to the future (e.g., "I'm unlovable; I'm incompetent; the world is dark; others can't be trusted"). These underlying core negative beliefs might make someone vulnerable to depression or anxiety.

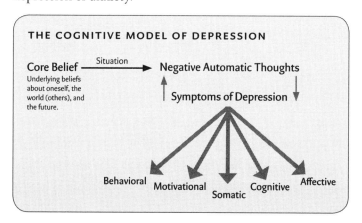

It is important to explain to your depressed clients that, in the cognitive behavioral model, the symptoms of depression are related to underlying thoughts that are activated by stressful life events.

The following are some common symptoms of depression:

• Problems with energy, appetite, and/or sleep (somatic symptoms)
• Sad or anxious feelings (affective or emotional symptoms)

- Lack of "oomph" or "get up and go" (motivational symptoms)
- Avoidance of contact with friends or family (behavioral symptoms)
- Negative thoughts related to oneself, the future, others, or the world (cognitive symptoms)

TWO DOMAINS OF NEGATIVE BELIEFS

Affiliative Domain
- "I am unlovable"
- "I am unworthy"
- "I am not good enough"
- "I am defective"

Achievement Domain
- "I am helpless"
- "I am powerless"
- "I am inadequate"
- "I am vulnerable"

According to the cognitive model, there are two domains of negative core beliefs that underlie automatic thoughts. Clients are thought to be vulnerable to depression because of negative thoughts or beliefs related to their lovability or their ability to achieve. To love and to work are critically important aspects of experience. An individual can be vulnerable in either or both of those domains. When working with clients, it is crucial to pay attention to automatic thoughts or core beliefs that relate to these themes. Is the vulnerability in the achievement domain, in the lovability (or affiliative) domain, or in both?

CBT TECHNIQUE

CBT TECHNIQUE DISTILLED TO ITS ESSENCE

- What is the client's most important problem to work on now?
- What cognitions and automatic thoughts are interfering with problem solving?
- What can I do to help the client see his or her problem in a more adaptive way and engage in more functional behavior?

What is cognitive therapy in action? The key question is what is the client's most important problem to work on now? And what are the thoughts that are interfering with your clients' ability to problem solve? Why can't your client handle the stressors that he is facing? Ask yourself, "What can I do to help the client see his situation in a more functional way and engage in more adaptive behavior?"

In every session, be active and work at the edge of your seat with your client to help him acquire skills to handle stress. Cognitive Behavioral Therapy is oriented to problem solving, and the goal of therapy is for clients to become their own therapists. This is accomplished by teaching them the cognitive model. This means identifying and modifying automatic thoughts, core beliefs, or behaviors through the use of the Automatic Thought Record, cognitive restructuring, and behavioral activation.

4 :: The Automatic Thought Record and Socratic Questioning

> ### CBT TECHNIQUES AND PRINCIPLES: THE AUTOMATIC THOUGHT RECORD
>
> - Identify problems and automatic thoughts
> - The Downward Arrow Technique
> - Socratic questioning
> - Cognitive restructuring

The Automatic Thought Record is a simple yet powerful tool and is the workhorse of CBT. It will be used in most sessions and will be frequently assigned as homework.

Work with clients to help them fill out the Automatic Thought Record, and subsequently assign it as homework. Begin with the first three columns by guiding clients to:

1. *Focus on and describe a specific situation* in which they experienced distress.
2. *Identify the emotions that they experienced in that situation.*
3. *Identify their automatic thoughts.* (Automatic thoughts are not always conscious.)

The following questions can help clients elicit automatic thoughts:

- "What was going through your mind just then?"
- "What were you thinking about just then, when you had this emotional shift?"
- "What did this situation mean to you, or mean about you, or mean about the future?"

If clients have difficulty identifying negative thoughts associated with the situation they have identified, then you might have to prompt them with an interpretation of what you think they might have been thinking. Invite them to confirm, disconfirm, correct, and clarify what they were thinking.

There are actually many different versions of Automatic Thought Records. The version we recommend is reprinted with permission from its creator, Dr. Christine Padesky, the coauthor with Dennis Greenberger of the very well-known CBT self-help book *Mind Over Mood* (Greenberger & Padesky, 1995). The Automatic Thought Record is laid out as a grid, with seven columns. You should use the first three columns during the early sessions. Later, after the client has acquired the skills necessary to complete the first three columns, you should then work on the next four columns.

When presenting the Automatic Thought Record, be sure to explain the cognitive model that links feelings with thoughts and behaviors as the underlying rationale for using this tool.

The first three columns involve identifying and focusing on a situation, the emotions or moods (including negative emotions) that occur in that situation, and the automatic thoughts associated with that negative shift in mood.

AUTOMATIC THOUGHT RECORD

Situation	Moods	Automatic Thought	Evidence that Supports the Hot Thought	Evidence that Doesn't Support the Hot Thought	Alternative Balanced Thought	Rate Mood
Thurs or Fri @8:20 AM: in bedroom, daughter comes, sees me crying; asks if she can help take care of baby	Helpless 80–90% Sad 90% Frustrated 50% Angry 30%	"This is it, game over" (I can't take care of my kids) . . . therefore "I'm a bad mother."				

© Center for Cognitive Therapy, www.padesky.com; Seven-Column Thought Record used with permission; © 1983 Christine A. Padesky, PhD.

When working on Column #3 of the thought record, it can be helpful to utilize the Downward Arrow Technique. This process of guided discovery can help to uncover deeper meanings or core beliefs that are triggered in specific situations. In using this simple method, you may stir up emotion for the client, but it is an opportunity for you to strengthen the therapeutic alliance. By responding in an empathic way, you can cement the therapeutic bond while helping the client to identify negative thoughts. This can enhance your mutual understanding of distressing experiences and underlying beliefs. For example, if a client tearfully states, "I'm unlovable; I'll always be alone," you can empathically respond in a validating manner: "I can see how emotional it is for you to be talking about these underlying thoughts and beliefs. This is important for us to understand and focus on in order to help you with this depression."

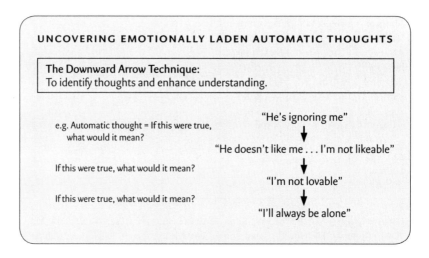

UNCOVERING EMOTIONALLY LADEN AUTOMATIC THOUGHTS

The Downward Arrow Technique:
To identify thoughts and enhance understanding.

e.g. Automatic thought = If this were true, what would it mean?

If this were true, what would it mean?

If this were true, what would it mean?

"He's ignoring me"
↓
"He doesn't like me . . . I'm not likeable"
↓
"I'm not lovable"
↓
"I'll always be alone"

The Downward Arrow Technique works as follows: in response to a client's automatic negative thoughts, ask him or her "If it were true, what would that mean to you?" or "If it were true, what would be the worst thing about that for you?" This can uncover emotionally charged underlying beliefs and fears; this helps get to the crux of the matter.

SOCRATIC QUESTIONING

> ### SOCRATIC QUESTIONING
>
> "In the best cognitive therapy there are no answers, only good questions that guide the discovery of a million different individual answers.
> There are questions that assume one truth versus questions that promote true discovery."

Once you have identified negative thoughts or core beliefs associated with a client's more intense emotions, the next step is to help her change that perspective, see her situation differently, and perceive herself differently. To do that we use an approach called Socratic questioning, or guided discovery. Socratic questioning is all about asking good questions that promote discovery and enhance awareness. We use it in order to complete the last four columns of the Automatic Thought Record and during therapy sessions.

As the cognitive therapist Christine Padesky has said, "In the best cognitive therapy there are no answers, only good questions that guide the discovery of a million different individual answers. There are questions that assume one truth versus questions that promote true discovery." The latter are the kinds of questions you want to ask with your client in CBT.

Unfortunately, supportive comments may not be sufficiently effective in helping your clients. Simply disagreeing when a client says something negative about himself or the world or about the future may not help him in the long run. There is nothing wrong with being supportive and saying kind things; however, this does not exemplify the CBT technique of Socratic questioning.

SOCRATIC QUESTIONING EXAMPLES

Situation: Depressed mother says, "I'm a complete failure."

- What makes you think you are a complete failure?
- How strongly do you believe this idea now?
- On a scale of 0–100% where do you fall?
  Where do other people fall?
- What would a "good mother" do?
- How does viewing yourself as a complete failure impact how you feel and act?

Socratic questioning requires sensitivity and creativity in order to help clients consider other ways of thinking. Some examples of exploratory questions that can be asked through this process are listed above. In gaining new perspectives, clients will be able to generate alternative ways of thinking and behaving to better cope with their situations.

5 :: Cognitive Restructuring

> **FIVE BASIC COGNITIVE RESTRUCTURING STRATEGIES**
>
> 1. Operationalize the negative thought
>   ("How do you define a bad mother?")
> 2. Evaluate the utility, implications, advantages, and
>   disadvantages of the thought or belief
> 3. Evaluate the accuracy of the belief (evidence for and against)
> 4. Evaluate the alternative ways of thinking in this situation
>   ("What would you say to a friend?")
> 5. Label the cognitive error (David Burn's List)

Cognitive restructuring strategies help clients to think about situations differently. Several are outlined above.

Operationalize the negative thought. Ask the client for examples or to define a generalized statement. In so doing, you can get at the client's underlying implicit beliefs and rules.

Evaluate the utility, the implications, the advantages, and the disadvantages of the thought. Get the client to consider how this thought serves him. What are the implications of thinking this way? What will happen if you think this way? You want to make thinking this way something that the client starts to see as maladaptive or unproductive. He needs to see the "cost" of thinking this way.

Evaluate the accuracy of the belief. Although this is a common and helpful therapeutic strategy, be sure to use a combination of cognitive restructuring strategies. Problems are a result not only of the inaccuracy of beliefs but also of the beliefs' poor utility and negative impact. Looking at the evidence for and against negative thinking can be quite powerful, especially when clients start to see that the evidence supporting their negative belief or thought is weak and that, in fact, there is a lot of evidence against their negative thinking.

Toward the end of a session in working through a problem, **help the client to see an alternative way or thought around the situation.** How might they think to themselves in a more productive way and self-coach themselves? We often ask, "What would be something you would say to a friend in the same situation?" Many times your client would be much more compassionate and helpful toward a close friend than toward himself. We want clients to align how they treat themselves with how they would treat others.

Another useful cognitive restructuring technique is to **look at thoughts more like ideas that may not be true.** Clients can start to objectify their thoughts by **classifying them as cognitive errors.** We often use David Burns's list of cognitive distortions or errors. Look at the list, refer to it, and learn some of the definitions for cognitive distortions, many of which overlap. These can then be gently challenged through the cognitive restructuring techniques. Below are a few very common and important cognitive errors.

"All or nothing" thinking, or dichotomous thinking, involves seeing the world in extremes (i.e., either black or white, with no shades of gray). For example, a client might think, "I'm either a loser or a winner. . . . I'm either lovable or unlovable." That kind of thinking can get her into hot water, especially if she experiences setbacks.

Catastrophizing is a kind of jumping to conclusions where clients expect the worst and subjectively interpret a negative situation in a way that is much worse than it is objectively.

Should/must statements are associated with putting unrealistically high

> ### DAVID BURN'S LIST OF COGNITIVE DISTORTIONS
>
> - All or nothing (dichotomous/black or white)
> - Catastrophizing
> - Disqualifying the positive
> - Emotional reasoning
> - Labeling
> - Magnification/minimization
> - Mental filter
> - Mind reading
> - Jumping to conclusions
> - Overgeneralizing
> - Should/must statements

expectations on oneself with harsh or unrelenting standards. This can be a recipe for guilt, for becoming psychologically paralyzed, for procrastinating, and for not being able to cope with situations.

When needed, refer back to David Burns's book *The Feeling Good Handbook* (1999) in order to identify other problematic patterns of thinking, which can then be changed.

The last four columns of the Automatic Thought Record are used to cognitively restructure the hot thought, defined as the most distressing or upsetting of the thoughts listed, and generate an alternative, more balanced, and adaptive way of thinking. This is done by exploring evidence that supports the hot thought; explaining evidence that does not support the hot thought; operationalizing the negative thought; evaluating the utility, implications, advantages, and disadvantages of the thought; evaluating the accuracy of the belief (evidence for and against); and labeling the cognitive error (using David Burns's list).

AUTOMATIC THOUGHT RECORD

Situation	Moods	Automatic Thought	Evidence that Supports the Hot Thought	Evidence that Doesn't Support the Hot Thought	Alternative Balanced Thought	Rate Mood
Thurs or Fri @8:20 AM: in bedroom, daughter comes, sees me crying; asks if she can help take care of baby	Helpless 80–90% Sad 90% Frustrated 50% Angry 30%	"This is it, game over" (I can't take care of my kids) . . . therefore "I'm a bad mother."	–I have trouble keeping things on schedule. –Daughter saw me crying, can't keep her safe. –Get impatient with kids. –I should be able to just snap out of it.	–Kids are happy most of the time. –They are major focus of my life. –There's a lot to do in a day, impossible to do everything. –Emotions are part of being a human being.	–It's ok to feel things. Just because my daughter may see that I am a human being doesn't mean that everything is falling apart or that I'm a bad mother.	Sadness 30%

© Center for Cognitive Therapy, www.padesky.com; Seven-Column Thought Record used with permission; © 1983 Christine A. Padesky, PhD.

Cognitive restructuring techniques are integrated within the process of completing Columns #4 and #5. Through this process of exploration, the client then generates alternative ways of thinking in this specific situation (Column #6). Here is where you might ask, "What would you say to a friend?"

Finally, have the clients re-rate their mood to see if there is any shift from the second column when they initially rated their mood. The hope is that the negative mood state would decrease in intensity by the end of this exercise. The mood may not diminish to zero, and that is fine. Clients may not be completely feeling okay about a stressful situation or about the adversity in their lives, but hopefully they will have fewer negative mood states, fewer negative emotions, and better outlooks on their situations. That's a sign that the Automatic Thought Record has worked. This can be powerfully reinforcing.

6 :: CBT Homework and Behavioral Therapeutic Strategies

EFFECTIVE CBT HOMEWORK

- Provide rationale
- Work collaboratively, not prescriptively
  - Use Socratic questioning to elicit suggestions from the patient
- Personalize the homework task to the client's abilities, needs, therapy goals, etc. (recalibrate if necessary)
- Start where the client is, not where the client thinks he or she should be
  - Be specific and concrete
  - Where, when, with whom, for how long, etc.

Cognitive Behavioral Therapy is a skill-based therapy. Learning any skill requires practice, and the way we get our clients to learn and practice in CBT is by giving homework. Here are a few tips to make homework as effective as possible. First, provide a rationale. If you tell people to do something and they are not quite sure why they are doing it, they are much less likely to learn from it or even to attempt the task. Collaboratively negotiate with clients to find homework tasks suitable to their level, something that they understand, with a reason or rationale behind tasks that they are doing.

Personalize homework tasks and make sure that they will be possible for clients to accomplish. Sometimes clients have lofty goals in terms of where they'd like to be, and that is something we encourage, but it is more feasible to reach a goal if it is done in a stepwise fashion. That means assigning homework tasks that may seem a little simple or basic. Gradually, over time, clients can gain confidence and come closer to meeting goals that they have set for themselves.

Finally, and perhaps most important, be as specific as possible with homework tasks. If you are vague or ambiguous, something is likely to go wrong. Clarify what time of day the task will be done at, and specify the days that will apply. What exactly will the client record or pay attention to? How long is this task going to last? Anticipate and make contingency plans in the event of difficulties. If there is some kind of interference, what might the client do instead, or how might she overcome the obstacle?

The more you adhere to these principles, the more likely your client will accomplish her homework task and benefit from the skills you are trying to teach.

ACTIVITY SCHEDULING/TIME MANAGEMENT

- Monitor
- Deliberately plan ahead
- Conduct behavioral experiments (e.g., pleasure predicting)
- Cognitive rehearsal: plan a list of successful steps, anticipate potential problems, generate solutions or contingency plans

Activity scheduling can improve the clients' subjective sense of well-being, help with the development of new skills, mitigate social isolation, and serve as a good distraction from ruminative worry.

Collaboratively and strategically plan for clients to do something that is feasible and might bring them a sense of accomplishment, a sense of mastery, or a sense of pleasure. Examples include going for a walk around the block or even activities such as doing the dishes. Give your clients a calendar that contains the days of the week as well as the hours of the day, and get them to write in exactly what it is that they want to do when. Then, in addition to recording the specific activities done, ask clients to record their sense of mastery and/or their sense of pleasure. Their sense of mastery has to do with how well they think they have accomplished the task. Their sense of pleasure has to do with how much they enjoyed the task. For example, doing laundry for most people doesn't bring a lot of pleasure, but at least one has a sense of accomplishment that one has put a dent in that dirty laundry pile. Conversely, there are activities such as watching a movie that may bring some pleasure but that don't necessarily involve a sense of mastery. Recording these two elements is important in giving the client an incentive to continue engaging in these kinds of activities.

As much as possible, develop contingency plans. Maybe the client plans to go for a walk every day at 9:00 a.m., but some days there are childcare issues and he is not able to go for a walk. It is to the client's benefit to plan in advance of these potential obstacles so that success is more likely. An alternate plan can be chosen, such as a different time, a different strategy, or a different day, all of which are negotiated with the client.

> **GRADED TASK ASSIGNMENT AND PROBLEM-SOLVING TECHNIQUES**
>
> - Simplify global problems into specific component tasks
> - The client first works on mastering the smaller components before moving on to try the more difficult elements of the problem
> - Define the problem, plan alternative solutions, evaluate likely consequences, select an optimal solution, prepare, implement the solution, reevaluate the outcome

Another common CBT behavioral technique is **graded task assignment**, or simply breaking down complex problems into smaller ones. Aaron T. Beck is fond of saying, "A journey of 1,000 miles begins with a single step," and that's certainly true in CBT. When tasks seem overwhelming, ask questions that help clients to problem solve the many small steps that can accomplish their tasks. Divide a larger task into small components that are easily achievable. Clients not only engage more fully with life but also achieve an increased sense of mastery in terms of what they are able to do in the context of their illness.

What are you going to do with your clients tomorrow or the next day in your own offices? How are you going to help them?

1. Track symptoms by using self-report questionnaires such as the Beck Depression or Anxiety Scales, and look at problems over time.
2. Use the Automatic Thought Record to collaboratively focus with

your clients on specific situations associated with negative emotions, and identify the associated automatic thoughts that go with those negative emotions. Work initially with the first three columns of the thought record, using the Downward Arrow Technique to identify underlying core beliefs. Assign the first three columns of the thought record as homework in the first few sessions and review it at every session.

3. Subsequently, use the whole thought record with your clients, teaching them how to fill out the thought record on their own. Help your clients to start to challenge their negative thoughts by using Socratic questioning to come up with alternative, more balanced thoughts.

4. Work with your clients in order to generate useful homework that will help them to acquire skills and to activate themselves to problem solve various situations in their day-to-day lives.

NEXT STEPS: WITH YOUR CLIENTS . . .

- Track symptoms and problems over time
- Focus on specific situations associated with negative emotions and identify associated automatic thoughts
- Use the Automatic Thought Record
- Use Socratic questioning to identify alternative thoughts and cognitively restructure in order to alleviate symptoms
- Collaboratively generate homework to activate clients and problem solve

7 :: Concluding Remarks

1. Always begin therapy by having clear goals: begin with the end goal in mind.

2. Try to illustrate the cognitive model whenever possible by taking global problems/issues and focusing on specific situations, emotions, and thoughts. The cognitive model will always take care of you therapeutically when you follow this strategy.

3. Emphasize teaching clients an adaptable general methodology to deal with emotional problems rather than solving their specific problems. Always ask clients what they learned when they feel better. This will help prevent relapses.

4. You must understand before you try to be understood: accurate empathy and a strong therapeutic relationship are critical before you apply CBT techniques such as cognitive restructuring. Don't jump in

prematurely to fix problems before you fully understand the client's world.

5. Teach clients how to complete the Automatic Thought Record in a graded task manner: complete the first three columns; then, only after mastery of this, complete all seven columns.

6. When assigning CBT homework, carefully calibrate the challenge: start where the client really is, not where he or she expects to be.

7. One behavioral experiment is worth 100 Automatic Thought Records: durable emotional change occurs through actual corrective experiences that disconfirm expectancies rather than through cognitive restructuring in isolation.

Lesson Plans

(See Appendix C for answers.)

LESSON PLAN #1
Reviewing Cognitive Techniques for Depression
Identify thoughts and emotions and review the first three columns of the
Automatic Thought Record
Watch Role Play #1 on the DVD

A. Discussion
1. What information goes into Column #1 of the Automatic Thought Record?
2. List two reasons the information in Column #1 should be as specific as possible.
3. What information goes into Column #2?
4. Why are the intensity ratings important?

5. Is suicidality an emotion or a thought?

6. Why is this an important distinction?

7. What is the "hot thought"?

8. What are ways to empathically respond to distress or tearfulness during a session?

9. List three techniques for helping a client to identify a hot thought.

10. Setting aside any other CBT techniques, how do you imagine that just being aware of your thoughts and emotions might be helpful or challenging?

11. Where do automatic thoughts come from?

B. Experiential Tasks

1. Set an alarm to go off at 6 minutes into the video. At that moment, pay attention to and write down your feelings and thoughts. Be thorough. What do you notice? Is there a connection between the thoughts and emotions? What might help you practice this skill of being more aware of thoughts and feelings?

2. Imagine that you are working with a client on a thought record (or you can work with a colleague or a friend). Carefully and slowly complete the first three columns. You may use an actual client complaint or a common work stressor such as not having enough work-life balance, being behind on paperwork, or feeling unhelpful or unskilled as a therapist. Make sure you identify and circle the "hot thought." If working in a pair, swap roles after 10

minutes. Once both of you have tried each role, compare and
review experiences.

C. **Homework**

Complete **the first three columns of the thought record** on at least
three different occasions when you notice a change in emotion. Try
to complete the thought records as close in time to the emotional
shift as you can. Pay attention to what you notice about the task and
any patterns that may emerge between the three thought records. Be
prepared to discuss these during the next session.

LESSON PLAN #2

Reviewing Cognitive Techniques for Depression
Examine the evidence and the last four columns of the thought record
Watch Role Play #2 on the DVD

Review Homework from Lesson Plan #1

A. **Discussion**

1. What is the difference between thoughts and evidence?
2. Why do we collect "evidence"?
3. How do you construct the balanced, alternative thought in
   Column #6 of the thought record?
4. Why do we re-rate moods in the last column?
5. Other than using the thought record, what are two other ways of
   modifying dysfunctional thoughts?

6. What can you do if there is no convincing evidence for or against a particular thought?

7. Why is it usually easier for clients to identify "evidence for" compared to "evidence against"?

8. What are two explanations for no mood change at the end of a thought record?

9. Why are there usually patterns to thought records that emerge over time?

10. How do you think underlying core beliefs or schemas are generated?

B. Experiential Tasks

1. Examine the evidence for and against this project being a useful exercise.

2. On your own, or with a colleague or friend, work through a thought record. Carefully and slowly complete the last four columns. You may continue to use your previous role play, starting with the hot thought you had already generated. Alternatively, you may begin with a hot thought such as "This is a waste of time" or "I'll never be a competent CBT therapist" or "I'm a terrible parent." If working in a pair, swap roles after 10 minutes. Once both of you have tried each role, compare and review experiences.

C. Homework

Complete all seven columns of the thought record on at least three different occasions when you notice a change in emotion. Try to complete the thought records as close in time to the emotional shift as you can. Pay attention to what you notice about the task and any patterns that may emerge between the three thought records. Pay particular attention to the ease or difficulty of generating evidence. Be prepared to discuss these during the next session.

LESSON PLAN #3
Reviewing Behavioral Techniques for Depression
Watch the portion of the DVD on behavioral techniques: Role Play #3

Review Homework from Lesson Plan #2

A. Discussion
1. What are three common behavioral coping strategies employed by clients who are suffering from untreated depression?
2. How do you understand these behaviors based on the cognitive model?
3. What are two behavioral strategies designed to help clients with depression?
4. What is the difference between "mastery" and "pleasure"? What are three examples of tasks that might be rated more highly in one category over another?
5. How does CBT help clients who do not feel able to accomplish a behavioral task?
6. How might you respond to a client who says that spending time with people "won't help anyways"?
7. How might you respond to a client who engages in a behavioral

task, such as going for a walk, but reports no pleasure from the activity?

8. Can clients engage in behavioral tasks with friends or family?

9. How would you respond to clients who are tired from their depression and who complain about their inability to perform tasks as efficiently as they used to do before they became ill?

10. How can you make use of an activity log in which clients report activities that unexpectedly bring them pleasure?

B. Experiential Tasks

1. Either by yourself or working with a colleague or friend, engage in a role play in which you work with a client who never leaves home and is isolated. Try to develop a plan to help the client engage in a small, manageable task before the next session. Be sure to look at any potential challenges/obstacles. If working in a pair, swap roles after 10 minutes. Once both of you have tried each role, compare and review experiences.

2. Try to come up with at least two specific times when you predicted an event would be less enjoyable than it ended up being and two specific times when you predicted an event would be more enjoyable than it ended up being. Reflect on how your thoughts affected your predictions. Reflect on why the predictions were not completely accurate.

C. Homework

Make a specific prediction about how pleasurable an activity will be this week. The activity may be something like completing paperwork or going to a social event or reading a book. Engage in that activity for one continuous hour over the course of the week. Rate your pleasure from o to 100 before the activity begins and then at 10-minute intervals until the end of the activity. Pay attention to any variation in pleasure and compare your ratings to your initial predictions. Be prepared to discuss these in the next session.

LESSON PLAN #4
Consolidation and Clinical Applications

Review Homework from Lesson Plan #3

A. Discussion

Case #1: A Case of Depression and Cognitive Distortions

Mrs. Claire Deloraine is a 42-year-old woman who works as a fourth-grade schoolteacher. She has worked in the same school for 13 years and has received several teaching awards during that time. She has been married to her husband, Charlie, a factory worker, for 12 years, and they have a 4-year-old boy and 1½-year-old twin girls. After the twins were born, Claire had thoughts of being overwhelmed but managed to cope as a stay-at-home mom with the help and support of Charlie. Claire went back to work in September and since then has been feeling extremely guilty about the decision to put her children in the local daycare.

She has begun to experience symptoms of depression over the last 6 weeks including tearfulness, low mood, low energy, anhedonia (a lack of pleasure in things), and decreased appetite. She has no suicidal ideation although she has recently begun to wonder if her family would be "better off" without her. Charlie takes the kids to daycare at 8 a.m. before work, and Claire picks them up after school at 4 p.m. She is always fearful the children will be angry with her at the end of the day, but they always come running toward her and give her a big hug.

She reports thoughts such as "I'm a terrible mother" and "I've abandoned my children." Charlie has been extremely supportive and would like to help, but his shift work prevents him from being home before 8 p.m. As a result, the rest of the family generally eats without him. Claire on several occasions has said, "It's like being a single mom." Although the children are all thriving, given her line of work, she has begun to worry about the long-term impact of this parenting arrangement on the children. She says, "They'll grow up feeling aban-doned" and "they'll never amount to anything with parents like us."

Case #1

1. What cognitive distortions is Claire employing? (Use David Burns's list as a reference.)
2. What evidence might you help Claire generate to counter some of her dysfunctional beliefs?
3. Will CBT make her feel 100% comfortable about her kids being in daycare?
4. How might defining "a good mother" be helpful in this case?
5. How might you use the fact that Claire is a schoolteacher to therapeutic advantage?

Case #2: A Case of Depression and Behavioral Activation

> *Bob Atkinson is a 63-year-old retired engineer. He worked for the same company for 40 years before accepting an early retirement package last year. Bob is not married and has no children. He had been dating a woman for about 2 years, but that relationship ended 6 months after Bob retired because he "didn't live his own life anymore."*
>
> *Over the last 4 months, Bob has become increasingly socially isolated. He no longer sees his work colleagues and has stopped returning his friends' calls. Whereas he used to swim daily, he has stopped completely. Bob used to eat in a very healthy fashion, stopping by the grocery store on the way home each day from work; however, over the past several months he has increasingly begun to rely on canned goods and pizza because he has lost interest in cooking. He reports thoughts like "what's the point in going out" or "I'm useless now, just living out my time . . . which probably won't be very long."*
>
> *Bob acknowledges that he spends most days in bed napping. While in bed he thinks about how he used to be a productive member of society, but now, "I'm just a mooch living off my retirement package."*

Case #2

1. What do you imagine are some of the cognitions behind Bob's interpersonal isolation?
2. How would you design a task around healthier eating?
3. How would you deal with Bob's noncompliance with the homework you assign him?

4. How would you convince Bob to get out of bed?

5. What specific behaviors might help Bob in this situation?

B. **Experiential Tasks**

1. What would you say to describe the key aspects of the cognitive model to a client with depression?

2. What will you do to help review/consolidate the skills you have learned over the last several weeks?

3. What are three techniques you could easily incorporate into your practice and try by next week?

4. Set specific homework tasks using CBT techniques to try and maintain skills or enhance learning.

Quiz

(See Appendix C for answers.)

Please complete the following 25 questions on Cognitive Behavioral Therapy for depression to the best of your knowledge. Answer as quickly as you can. There is only ONE correct response for each question—choose the best answer for each question.

1. List at least five key principles or characteristics of cognitive therapy treatment.

    • _____

    • _____

    • _____

    • _____

    • _____

2. Which of the following is an example of cognition?
   a. Anxious or depressed feelings
   b. Automatic thoughts
   c. Negative behaviors
   d. Somatic symptoms

3. Helpful techniques that are taught in cognitive therapy include:
   a. Directional change
   b. Examining the evidence
   c. Activity analysis
   d. Emotional reasoning

4. Automatic thoughts can be described as:
   a. Out of your control
   b. Usually rational
   c. Usually caused by unhappy feelings
   d. Private

5. Which of the following is an example of an emotion?
   a. Thinking you're not good enough
   b. Wanting to give up
   c. Reacting with sadness
   d. Deciding not to show your fear

6. Which of the following is not written down in the Automatic Thought Record?
   a. Unconscious thoughts

b. Evidence for and against thoughts

c. Emotions

d. Events/situations

7. Mr. R, a salesman, was performing about 10% below his sales target for the year. The problem was largely due to an economic downturn in his region of the country. Although his job wasn't really threatened and his family relationships were in good shape, Mr. R began to think "Everything is falling apart—I'll lose it all." What kind of mistake in thinking might he be having?

    A. Overgeneralization

    B. Mind reading

    C. Ignoring the evidence

    D. Catastrophizing

a. A and C

b. B and D

c. A, C, and D

d. All of the above

8. Mr. R (the salesman described in the previous question) decided to start cognitive therapy. Which of these techniques do you think might help him?

a. Emotional reasoning

b. Programming

c. Denying automatic thoughts

d. Labeling cognitive errors or distortions

9. Ms. T has a number of long-standing negative core beliefs such as "I'll never succeed" and "I have to be perfect to be accepted." No matter how hard she tries, she always seems to think that she is "not measuring up." Which cognitive therapy procedure do you think might help her?

    a.   Listing advantages and disadvantages

    b.   Activation

    c.   Telling her that her thoughts are making her feel worse

    d.   Relaxation

10. Mr. G has been feeling depressed and has withdrawn from most of the activities that he used to enjoy. It seems like nothing gives him pleasure anymore. What would you recommend that he do to improve his mood?

    a.   Stay away from all stressful situations

    b.   Use an activity schedule, recording levels of mastery and pleasure

    c.   Don't push for change until he starts to feel better

    d.   Reassure himself that this will change

11. Which of the following statements does NOT accurately describe core beliefs?

    a.   They often stimulate automatic thoughts.

    b.   They can act as underlying rules.

    c.   They are upsetting emotions.

    d.   They can be very helpful.

12. A client with moderate major depression comes to you for advice about the optimal treatment for his condition. He has no medical problems that are contributing to his condition. He tells you that he would ideally prefer an antidepressant treatment found to be effective from research studies and he does not want to take medication. He also would like a treatment that will protect him against relapse. What of the following would you NOT tell him about CBT?

    a. He should try a course of CBT because it has been shown to be as effective as medication over the long term for mild to moderate depression.
    b. CBT is structured and time-limited.
    c. CBT focuses on thoughts, feelings, and behaviors.
    d. CBT focuses on relationships and the unconscious.

13. Regarding the basic cognitive model, which of the following statements is incorrect?

    a. People have more control over their feelings than their thoughts and behaviors.
    b. Thoughts, feelings, and behaviors are interconnected.
    c. People have more control over thoughts and behaviors than their feelings.
    d. Automatic thoughts come from the activation of core beliefs.

14. Characteristics of core beliefs include all of the following, EXCEPT that:

    a. Some relate to affiliation

b. Some are genetic

c. Some relate to achievement

d. Some are about the self

15. What is the most popular tool used in CBT to help clients learn to identify and ultimately challenge their negative thinking?

a. The activity log

b. The Beck Depression Inventory

c. The Automatic Thought Record

d. David Burns's cognitive distortions

16. Behavioral techniques that are utilized in CBT include all of the following, EXCEPT:

a. Activity scheduling

b. Asking friends and family to remind you to cheer up

c. Self-monitoring

d. Evaluating a sense of mastery or pleasure

17. Regarding the cognitive model of depression, all of the following are true EXCEPT that:

a. Core beliefs cause stressful events

b. Automatic thoughts develop and can be linked to negative core beliefs

c. Automatic thoughts can lead to somatic symptoms

d. Symptoms of depression are directly linked to negative automatic thoughts

18. All of the following are true about the Automatic Thought Record, EXCEPT:
    a. It is a commonly used tool in CBT
    b. It can work effectively only if the client completes all seven columns
    c. It can help the client learn how to identify automatic thoughts
    d. It can help the client learn how to challenge automatic thoughts

19. Your client describes spending most of her day in bed and has become socially isolated since becoming depressed. You are trying to help her to become more behaviorally activated. When explaining her homework, you mention all of the following, EXCEPT:
    a. The rationale for the homework
    b. Contingency planning
    c. That the homework will be viewed as successful if she experiences a decrease in symptoms as a result
    d. The reiteration of a feasible plan with specific details

20. All of the following are cognitive restructuring techniques, EXCEPT:
    a. Asking the client to do the opposite of her negative thought
    b. Examining the utility of the automatic negative thought
    c. Examining the evidence for and against the negative thought
    d. Asking her what she would say to a friend

21. By explaining depression to a client, we relate the symptoms of depression to underlying thoughts triggered by stressful life events.

Which of the following lists correctly provides examples of symptoms of depression?

a. Motivational symptoms, such as problems with energy, appetite, or sleep

b. Somatic symptoms, such as lacking the "oomph" to get out of bed to do things

c. Behavioral symptoms, such as avoiding contact with friends or family

d. Emotional symptoms, such as negative thoughts related to oneself, the world, and the future

22. Activity scheduling is a way of getting people who are stuck at home, because of depression or anxiety, to get out and start to do other things. It performs the following functions:

   A. It acts as a distraction.

   B. Clients may learn something new from the experience.

   C. Clients may develop a slightly stronger sense of being able to cope with their illness.

   D. Clients may feel a bit better.

a. A and C

b. B and D

c. A, C, and D

d. All of the above

23. The CBT technique of a graded task assignment involves:

A. Breaking down complex or overwhelming problems into smaller ones
B. Focusing on the enormity of tasks
C. Asking questions that help clients to problem solve
D. Helping clients to gain an increased sense of affiliation in terms of their relationships in the context of their illness

a. A and C
b. B and D
c. A, B, and D
d. All of the above

24. Which of the following is NOT true of the Downward Arrow Technique?
a. It can be helpful in discovering the deeper meanings or core beliefs that are triggered in a situation.
b. A clinician asks about a thought or belief, "If that were true what would that mean to you?"
c. It can provide an opportunity for empathic validation.
d. In stirring strong negative emotions, it weakens the therapeutic alliance.

25. Cognitive therapy focuses on
a. Changing the views that people take of things
b. Changing the feelings that people have about things
c. Changing the symptoms that people have when they suffer from depression
d. Changing the views that family members have about clients

Appendix A:
Role-Play Transcripts

(Refer to the enclosed DVD for the full video.)

Clare is a 36-year-old married mother of three children who came to your office at the suggestion of her family doctor. She has struggled with depression since the birth of her youngest child, around 2 years ago. Although she was started on an antidepressant medication, it has only partially remitted her symptoms. She has not struggled with suicidal ideation; however, she continues to feel overwhelmed and has low self-esteem, difficulties with motivation and energy, and episodic tearfulness associated with low mood. Her mother struggled with depression as well and Clare has expressed worries that she is becoming a nonfunctioning parent for her kids, which is similar to what she grew up with. She has said, "I don't want to be that parent."

ROLE PLAY #1:
AUTOMATIC THOUGHT RECORD (COLUMNS #1–3)

In the first role play, Dr. Ari Zaretsky illustrates how one works with a client by focusing on a specific situation to identify the emotions and the automatic thoughts with an Automatic Thought Record. [Please note the captions from the video presentation are bolded in the following text at the points at which they appear.]

THERAPIST: Hi Clare, why don't we set an agenda for today. What would you like to focus on today?

CLIENT: I don't know, I guess I'm just feeling . . . like, I don't know why I don't feel better than I do. I've been taking this medication and I feel a little better but I feel like I have no reason to feel how I'm feeling. I should feel fine. I've got a wonderful family. I really don't have anything to feel this way about and I can't seem to make it go away.

T: You can't seem to make yourself feel better.

C: M'hmm.

[Introducing the Automatic Thought Record]

T: Looking at your Beck Depression Inventory it certainly seems that things are far from good. Even though the medication is helping a little bit, I see a lot of depressive symptoms and it appears that you're still having problems with fatigue and low energy and a lot of self-criticism, and clearly we still have a lot of work to do together to make you feel better. So why don't we get started with that? One of the things that I wanted to do today is actually to help you get more of a handle on your negative thinking, because we've identified that's one of the issues, right? You're having a lot of negative thoughts, a lot of hopelessness, a lot of self-criticism, and I'm wondering if we could go through the first three columns of the thought record. I mentioned earlier that one of the workhorses of our therapy is going to be the thought record and this is one of the tools that I'm going to teach you to become your own therapist. So I'd like to do that today, actually teach you how to fill out the first three columns of the thought record. Would you be open to that?

C: Yeah, I need to feel differently. I don't know; I'm open to anything, really.

[Identifying a specific emotionally charged situation]

T: Okay, well, what I thought we would do then is fill it out together and then you'll be able to use it and practice it on your own. So why don't we look at a situation where you noticed a real shift in your mood, where you noticed that you started to feel some negative feelings, something that came up recently, that you can think of that happened recently? Does anything come to mind that you can describe?

C: Well, I know last week I had an argument with my husband and afterwards I was crying and my daughter came in and saw me crying and that made me feel really . . . she just shouldn't see me like that.

T: It really touches a nerve for you even to talk about it right now, is that right?

C: Yeah.

T: Well, maybe we could focus on that situation since it does stir up a lot of feelings for you. What I'd like to do is actually give you the sheet and we'll fill it out together. So I'll take one sheet and you'll take the other and we'll go through it together.

C: Okay.

[Focusing on the details of the situation]

T: Can you describe to me in the first column—that's the situation—exactly what happened. Describe it almost in slow motion, like it's a film happening in slow motion. When was it that you started to feel these really intense feelings?

C: Well, we had had this argument and I just couldn't shake it. He had gone to work and . . .

T: So when was this exactly?

C: Last Thursday or Friday.

T: So it was last Thursday or Friday. Can you write that down?

C: Yeah.

T: Around what time was it?

C: It was about . . . we were just getting ready to leave for school so it was maybe about 8:20.

T: And can you describe again what happened with your daughter?

C: Well, the argument had happened a couple of hours before that. My husband was long gone, he leaves really early, but I just couldn't shake off how I was feeling. I went into the bedroom . . .

T: So you were in the bedroom.

C: I was in the bedroom and I was trying to get the baby, he had run in there, and I just couldn't stop crying. And she came in and she saw me crying and she was worried. She said, "Mommy, what's wrong?" and she thought maybe I was angry with her. And then she wondered if I wanted her to take care of the baby because then I could have a rest.

T: I see. So let's write this down then. So the situation last Thursday or Friday, it's around 8:20 in the morning, you're in your bedroom and your daughter comes in, and this is your 9-year-old, right?

c: Yeah.

t: Your 9-year-old daughter comes in and sees you crying and then asks you if you would like her to look after the baby, is that correct?

c: M'hmm.

t: And that's when things really hit you hard, is that right?

c: Yeah.

t: Okay. So do you see how we've written down the situation? We've tried to summarize the situation in a nutshell.

c: Yeah.

t: That's what I would want you to do outside of here.

c: Okay.

[Identifying the emotions associated with the situation]

t: So the next column is about moods. It's about the emotions that you experienced in that situation. So what emotions did you experience then?

c: I felt pretty helpless, really sad.

t: So, helpless, can you write that down, and sad. It's even touching a nerve for you now as we're talking about it.

c: Yeah.

t: Were there other feelings that you had in that situation?

c: I was frustrated with myself.

t: So, frustrated, can you write that down? Anything else that came up for you in terms of emotions?

c: I think mostly that. I was maybe a bit angry with myself for letting her see me like that.

t: So angry as well.

C: But mostly sad.

[Rating the intensity of emotions (0 to 100%)]

T: Mostly sad, okay, that's important. So the next step is actually to rate the intensity of these different emotions. You identified a number of different emotions. Let's go through it and rate the intensity on a scale of 0, not at all, to 100%, the most intense you've ever felt that emotion in your entire life. So the first thing you said is helpless, is that right?

C: Yeah.

T: How intense was the helplessness?

C: Maybe 8 or 9.

T: So maybe 80% or 90%, okay. And then what about sadness?

C: Nine or ten.

T: Okay, so 90% sad. And then what about frustrated, how intense was that on a scale of 0 to 100?

C: Maybe 50.

T: Fifty percent, somewhat less. And then angry, how intense was that on a scale of 0 to 100?

C: Maybe 30.

[Identifying automatic thoughts]

T: Okay, so 30%. So the next step is . . . we're in the third column and we want to identify the thoughts that you were having in that situation. Try to put yourself back there in your mind's eye. See it happening, your daughter talking to you, asking you about whether you want her to look after the baby, and then you start to feel these intense feelings. What do you think is going through your mind at that moment? What do you think you're saying to yourself?

c: This is it: game over.

t: So let's write that down, this is it: game over. Now, what I want to do with you right now is try to explore that a little bit further. What do you mean by that? What does that mean to you when you say, game over? Can you tell me a little bit more about what that means to you personally?

c: It means that . . . it means I can't take care of my kids.

[Using the Downward Arrow Technique to explore thoughts and underlying core beliefs]

t: So can you write that down? I wonder if we could explore that even further. Let's make another arrow that goes downward. What does that mean to you? If that was true, that you can't take care of your kids, what would be the worst thing about that for you? What would that mean to you?

c: That I'm a bad mother.

[Identifying which thought is most emotionally charged = the hot thought]

t: And that again touches a nerve for you, doesn't it? So I'm a bad mother. Given the way you're reacting right now, I'm wondering if that's a theme for you, an issue that's been going through your mind in the past?

c: I guess I just don't want to end up like my mother. I don't want my daughter to end up having to take care of me the way I had to take care of my mother.

t: Is that something that is familiar for you then, I'm a bad mother?

c: M'hmm.

t: That's something you say to yourself a lot?

c: I'm just . . . I guess sometimes I'm afraid I don't know how to be a good mother. I'm so afraid of messing it up, not getting it right.

[**Assigning homework: Fill out the Automatic Thought Record daily**]

T: One of the things I'd like to do then, to suggest to you, is for us to start to pay attention to this and to look at this across time, across different contexts, and I'm wondering if you'd be willing to fill this thought record out on a more frequent basis outside of here. I wonder if you would be willing to start to track whether you have negative thoughts like this in other situations and what comes up. Would you be open to that?

c: Yeah. Like I said, I'll really do anything. I just want to feel differently.

T: At the beginning you may find that as we do this it stirs up some feelings for you. My hope would be that over time, though, you'll have the skills that I'll teach you to be able to deal with these negative thoughts that come up.

c: Okay.

T: So the homework for you is to actually start to fill out this thought record, the first three columns, to take this with you and to start to fill it out on a daily basis based on situations that stir up negative feelings for you and let's see what comes up.

c: Okay.

ROLE PLAY #2:
COGNITIVE RESTRUCTURING USING THE
AUTOMATIC THOUGHT RECORD

This role play demonstrates the second part of working with an Automatic Thought Record, illustrating how one does cognitive restructuring. Socratic questioning, as guided discovery, is used to work with the client's negative thoughts to change the perspective and come up with adaptive homework for the client to engage in to better cope with the situation.

T: Clare, we've been working on the first three columns of the thought record and I'm wondering how the homework went.

C: Okay. I probably should have done it a little more than I did but I did manage to do it a fair bit. I guess it was sort of surprising to see that I am having a lot of negative thoughts. That was interesting.

[**Exploring themes to further clarify the hot thought for cognitive restructuring**]

T: Looking at this thought record that you gave me, what you had worked on for homework, I'm wondering if you see a theme here based on what we've been talking about.

C: Well, there was kind of a lot of stuff around mothering, for sure.

T: And what I see here in this thought record is this hot thought of, I'm a bad mother.

C: M'hmm.

T: And that seems to be a major thought for you that causes a lot of distress.

C: I guess I'm . . . I'm just really afraid of that. I'm really afraid of turning out to be a bad mother.

T: One of the things I want to do right now with you is to go through the rest of the thought record and focus on those other four columns. So I'm wondering if we could do that right now, because the goal is to teach you the skills to become your own therapist, to be able to talk to yourself in different situations when you're feeling distress. Would you be open to doing that with me right now?

C: Sure.

[Cognitive restructuring: Exploring evidence for negative automatic thoughts]

T: So we've identified this negative thought, I'm a bad mother, and I'm wondering what the evidence is that supports that hot thought.

C: I guess I have trouble sometimes keeping things on schedule.

T: Can you write that down?

C: M'hmm.

T: Let's make a list of all the things that you think relate to being a bad mother, that supports the sense that you're a bad mother.

C: Well, the time my daughter saw me crying.

T: So that's one instance you feel is important.

C: It makes me feel like I'm not . . . she can't be feeling safe. I should be providing a safe environment.

T: Are there other things that you also think are important in terms of the sense that you're a bad mother?

C: I don't know, sometimes I get short with them, get impatient maybe.

[Exploring evidence that doesn't support the automatic thought]

T: So you get impatient with your kids, okay. So we've listed a number of things that you feel are evidence to support this sense that you're a bad mother. I want to go into the next column and look at, is there any evidence that doesn't support this idea that you're a bad mother, that actually would disconfirm that sense that you're a bad mother?

c: I guess they're pretty happy most of the time.

t: So your kids are happy most of the time. How does that relate to your mothering, do you think?

c: Well, I hope it means I'm giving them what they need.

t: Can you write that down? Anything else that you can think of that goes against this sense that you're a bad mother?

c: They're kind of the main focus of everything, really.

t: They're really important to you, a major focus in your life.

c: M'hmm.

[Exploring alternative explanations to shift the client's perspective]

t: Okay. And let's look at some of the things you put down in the first column here about evidence that supports the negative thought that you're a bad mother, for example, the fact that you're not able to get some of these chores done. Is there another way to explain that besides being a bad mother? What would you say to a friend, for example, who was telling you this about her situation?

c: Well, I guess it depends. I'm home all day; I should be able to do it all.

t: Well, do you think that you would say that to a friend?

c: Probably not.

t: What kinds of things would you say to a friend who was going through the same situation as you?

c: There are so many things to do in a day. Sometimes it's impossible to get them all done.

T: Can you write that down?

C: In the same place?

T: M'hmm. This is the evidence that does not support this sense that you're a bad mother. You also mentioned that your daughter saw you crying and I'm wondering if there is another way to look at that situation besides this idea that you're a bad mother. Again, what might you say to a friend if their daughter had seen them crying?

C: I guess emotions are part of being a human being and just because people are big doesn't mean they don't have them.

T: So it's interesting, isn't it, that you are able to give some advice to a friend. How do you think that relates to you?

C: Like, the same advice, you mean?

T: M'hmm.

C: I guess my expectations for myself are that I get it right.

T: So that's interesting, isn't it, that you have this sense that you have to be different than your friend, that you would hold yourself to a higher standard than your friend, and I'm wondering if you see that as a theme for yourself, that you're really hard on yourself?

C: Yeah, I think I am.

[Identifying cognitive errors (i.e., using Burns's list]

T: Earlier we had talked about some of the cognitive errors that people make when they get depressed and one of them is "should" statements of how they should be, what they should do, and I'm wondering if this might be an example of a "should" statement, that I should never feel overwhelmed, I should never cry.

C: Yeah, I should just . . . like, sort of the way I'm feeling. I feel like I should be able to snap out of it.

T: So can you see that as a "should" statement, as something that may not be the most accurate way to look at things?

C: M'hmm.

[Cognitive restructuring: Generating an alternative, balanced automatic thought]

T: Can you write that down? Something like, this might be an example of a "should" statement. If you look at the whole picture now, looking at the evidence that you initially wrote down to support the hot thought and then the evidence that does not support the hot thought, I'm wondering if there's a way to put it all together and come up with an alternative way to talk to yourself, what you might say to a friend. In particular, a friend who might be experiencing depression, who might be on medication and is describing how they feel a bit better but not fully better, and then they describe this situation happening to them. What advice would you give your friend? What would you say to them in the end?

C: Oh, that it's okay to feel overwhelmed and they're big things that are hard to get over sometimes really quickly.

T: Your friend is saying that they are a bad mother. What would you say to them about this situation where their daughter saw them crying? How would you talk to your friend in this situation?

C: You're just expressing how you're feeling and your kids know that you love them and you're with them all the time. It's okay for them to see the cracks. It doesn't mean that everything is falling apart.

T: How much do you believe that right now, on a scale of 0 to 100?

C: For me or for them? For me or for my friend?

T: For you, how much do you believe that?

C: I think it may be possible to believe that. I don't know if I . . . I think the logic of it makes sense and I should probably think about that more.

T: So you somewhat believe it.

C: M'hmm.

T: You can see that perspective at least, is that right?

C: Yeah.

T: Okay, so, it's important to write that down as an alternative perspective and that would be in that second to last column, alternative balance thoughts, some of the things you talk about. Can you say it again?

C: It's okay to feel things. Just because she may see that you are a human being doesn't mean that everything is falling apart.

T: Okay. Just because she sees that you're a human being, that you have feelings, that you cry, doesn't mean that everything is falling apart. Or that you're a bad mother?

C: Okay.

[Cognitive restructuring: Re-rating mood to emphasize the potential benefits]

T: And when you say that right now to yourself, what kind of feelings do you have? I'm interested in particular in how that relates to the initial feelings that you had. So initially you described sadness 90%. What about now, as you say this to yourself?

C: Maybe 30.

T: Thirty percent, so can you write that in the last column—sadness, 30%. So that's really what we're doing. We're trying to go through a situation, we are trying to analyze your thoughts, and looking at the evidence for and the evidence against. We're trying to look at possible errors in the way you're thinking. We're trying to look at the way you might talk to a friend in the same situation, to try to generate another way to talk to yourself. Does that make sense to you?

C: Yeah, it does.

T: Do you think that you could do this on your own, outside of the session with me?

C: I could try.

T: Well, all you can do is try. And I'm wondering, for homework, if you'd be willing to start doing the full thought record in situations where, again, you notice a shift in your mood and start to experience negative feelings. Do you think you could write it down, write down the situation, write down your thoughts?

C: Yeah. Okay, great.

ROLE PLAY #3:
GRADED BEHAVIORAL TASK ASSIGNMENT

Dr. Mark Fefergrad performs a role play in which he helps the client to develop some behavioral tasks and to work on a graded task assignment.

T: Hi Clare. I know you've been in CBT for a few sessions now and you've been working very diligently on some of those thought records.

C: Yeah.

T: And I think that's really important. You may recall that negative thinking is closely associated with those low moods. But in CBT there is another component: that third corner of the triangle that's related to emotions and I wonder if you remember what that is?

c: Behavior.

T: That's absolutely right. So I thought today we might focus a little
bit on some of the behaviors and what kind of impact they might be
having on your mood. Would that be all right?

c: Sure.

[Activity scheduling: Exploring how time is spent in a typical day]

T: So I think the best way to approach this is, maybe you can tell me
a little bit about a standard day for you. How are you spending your
time during an average weekday?

c: Well, it's mostly about taking kids back and forth to school. I tend to
take them in the morning and then usually pick them up for lunch
and then again at the end of the day. So in between I've got the
2-year-old.

T: He's with you all the time, right?

c: Yeah, Sam's pretty busy so I sort of run around after him mostly in
the mornings, and then in the afternoon he has his nap and so do I.

T: It sounds like a pretty hectic schedule.

c: Well, you know, there are three of them. They're still little enough
that they need things from me. My daughter doesn't need as much.
She's starting to be more independent but . . .

T: I'm curious, you mentioned that in the afternoon your son has a nap
but you have a nap as well. Is that pretty consistent for you?

c: Yeah. I've been doing that for a while.

T: And about how long a nap is this, would you say?

c: A couple of hours maybe.

[Exploring thoughts and feelings associated with specific activities]

T: I'm always trying to make those connections in the CBT triangle. What kinds of thoughts do you have when you think about that nap time?

C: Well, I don't really . . . I guess I've just gotten into the habit of it. I don't really feel like doing anything. I'm so tired all the time. It just feels like the easiest thing to do. I guess I should be doing other things. It's probably why I'm not able to stay on top of things so well.

T: So I'm listening to you closely and it sounds like there are some negative thoughts associated with this nap. Maybe I should be doing other things. I wonder if actually having these naps might in some way be associated with your depression and I wonder what you think about that idea.

C: I guess. I've never really . . . I guess that's possible. I just feel so tired all the time and I don't really feel like doing things, so sleeping with him seems to be kind of an obvious choice. I know it would be time for me to get other things done.

[Exploring activities that are associated with feelings of pleasure or mastery]

T: Do you have some time during the day where either you're doing things that are pleasurable or enjoyable for you, or maybe getting some tasks done that you'd really like to get out of the way?

C: Not really. I mean, I tend to get a little bit done in the morning before we leave for school, and then I usually take him to the park for a little while so he can play. I don't know, and then it seems like it's time to pick the kids up. In the evenings I don't really feel like doing anything.

T: It sounds like you're doing lots of things for the kids, not so many things just for you, and I wonder if that's something that maybe we can work on together. Would that be all right?

c: Sure.

t: I wonder if maybe you're getting caught in one of these traps where depression, as you know, saps some of your energy and you are more inclined to sleep and rest. But that takes up some of your time during the day so you're not doing things for the household or for yourself and pretty soon you get caught in that kind of vicious cycle. And what I'm hoping is we might be able, together, to design a way to get you out of that cycle.

c: Okay.

[Brainstorming to generate ideas to behaviorally activate]

t: So, ideally, what I'd like to do is put some pleasure back in your life, and by that I mean, maybe we can take that nap time, which is a couple of hours, and decide on something together that might be more for you, something that's in line with what you'd like to do if you were more healthy. Can you think of anything, either that you've been wanting to do or maybe something that you used to do that you haven't been doing as often?

c: Well, I used to run with my husband and I really miss doing that, but he's way past me now. I haven't run since when I got pregnant and now he's running marathons so I would never be able to keep up, I don't think.

t: I think it's a fabulous idea. Running, as we know, works as an anti-depressant so that's good for your mood, it's good for your health. You'd potentially get to spend time with your husband, but it sounds like maybe running with him right off the bat is a little bit ambitious.

c: Yeah.

[Finding a feasible plan for action]

t: So what could you imagine that might be a little bit easier for you to accomplish, ultimately building up to that goal of running with your husband?

c: Maybe running on my own again.

t: I'm aware that you do have this 2-year-old with you.

c: Yeah.

t: And that's going to be a little bit tricky.

c: Well, I mean, I suppose I could walk at first, maybe.

[Making a specific feasible plan]

t: Walking before you run, I like that. So let's try and hammer out some of those specifics. You're talking about taking a walk. What kind of distance or length of time are you thinking about? What might be feasible given the amount of exercise you've done recently?

c: Which is zero. Maybe half an hour, 45 minutes.

t: Really, could you do that much?

c: Well, I could do a half hour.

t: Okay, let's keep it at a level that we're pretty sure you can do. So a half hour and that would be slotted into that nap time in the afternoon. And how are you going to bring your son along?

c: He still goes in the stroller.

t: So he might be able to have his regular nap in the stroller while you're getting your exercise.

c: Yeah.

t: That sounds like a marvelous idea. So I'm going to pin you down even further. You've talked about going for a half hour. Between now and next Wednesday, how many times do you think you might be able to go out on that half-hour walk?

c: Maybe twice.

t: Okay. And which days do you think? I want you to commit to some specific days where you might be able to do that.

c: Thursday is not great but Friday is good, and maybe Monday.

[Exploring foreseeable obstacles]

t: Friday and Monday, perfect. And we always want to try to foresee any obstacles that might occur. Is there anything that might go on or might get in the way that might prevent you from carrying out your plan on Friday or Monday?

c: Maybe bad weather or one of the kids getting sick.

t: Okay. So one of the kids getting sick, I understand that's a tough one. I wonder if there's any way around the weather, though.

c: Not so much. Well, I guess I could just bundle up.

[Homework: Recording activities and mood along with a sense of mastery or pleasure]

t: That would be fabulous. So it sounds like we've got the beginnings of a plan where this Friday and this Monday you're going to go for a half-hour walk with your son in the stroller, and I think whenever we do some kind of behavior in CBT it's important to record what kind of impact it had. So I'm going to ask you to write down a couple of things after each of these walks. The first is going to be related to your mood. That's something you're familiar with from the thought records. The second is some sense of mastery. The reason I bring that up is, sometimes when you're depressed you might not feel like you can do much. You might not feel that capable. But I have to say, being a mom who during the day is on her own taking care of herself but also taking care of her son, I wonder if there might be some increased sense of satisfaction or feeling a bit better about yourself if you were able to accomplish these tasks. So I'm going to propose that maybe we'll make a chart together where you can record some of these items, both before and after the walk. That will give us a bit of a sense as to whether or not things have changed. Do you think that's possible?

C: Sure.

T: Okay, excellent. I look forward to seeing you next Wednesday and hearing all about these walks.

C: Okay.

Appendix B:
Practice Reminder Summary

(Refer to the enclosed Practice Reminder Card.)

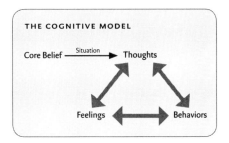

THE COGNITIVE MODEL

Core Belief ——— Situation ———▶ Thoughts

Feelings ◀——▶ Behaviors

OVERARCHING PRINCIPLES

1. Begin therapy with *clear goals*, and with "the end" in mind. Understand your clients *before* you expect to be understood by them. Accurate empathy and a strong therapeutic relationship are critically important to establish before you apply CBT techniques like cognitive restructuring. Don't jump in prematurely to fix problems before you fully understand the patient's world.

2. Take *global* problems or issues and focus on *specific* situations, emotions, and thoughts.

3. Emphasize teaching of an adaptable general method to deal with emotional problems rather than just solving the client's specific problem. Always ask what clients learned when they feel better.

4. *Track problems and symptoms over time.* Each session, use self-report questionnaires (i.e., Beck Depression or Anxiety Scales).

PSYCHOEDUCATION—THE CBT MODEL

5. **Thinking and behavior are the focus of CBT.** Every moment of our existence can be broken into three components that interact: thinking (cognitions, automatic thoughts, and core beliefs), feeling (emotions and mood), and actions or behavior (including physiological reactions, such as an increased heart rate).

Rationale for CBT—Explain to your clients:

- Thoughts and behaviors are the focus of CBT, because these can change. We can indirectly control our feelings by changing our thinking and behavior.
- Automatic thoughts are a result of underlying core beliefs related to themselves, the world, or the future.
- Symptoms of depression can be linked to thoughts and core beliefs that are activated by precipitating stressful life events.

DISCOVER:

i. What is the patient's most important problem to work on *now*?
ii. What are the thoughts that interfere with or get in the way of your client being able to problem solve?
iii. Why can't he handle the stressor that he is facing, the adversity in his life?
iv. How can you help your patient to see his situation and engage in behaviors that are more adaptive?

THE AUTOMATIC THOUGHT RECORD:
FIRST THREE COLUMNS

6. **Use the Automatic Thought Record in all sessions, review, and assign as homework.**

Look for patterns of core beliefs in the domains of lovability or achievement.

1. Collaboratively focus on a specific situation in which a client experiences distress.

2. Identify the emotions that she is experiencing in that situation.

3. Help her to identify and discover automatic thoughts, which are not always conscious. Use the Downward Arrow Technique to identify core beliefs, asking her, "If a specific automatic thought were true, what it would mean to them?"

Questions to identify automatic thoughts can include the following:
"What was going through your mind just then?"
"What do you think you were thinking about just then,
*   when you had this emotional shift?"*
"What did this situation mean to you or mean about you
*   or mean about the future?"*

THE AUTOMATIC THOUGHT RECORD: LAST FOUR COLUMNS

7. *Socratic questioning, or guided discovery,* helps clients to change thinking and behaviors in combination with homework (see below). Teach clients to fill out thought records on their own in order to challenge their negative thoughts and generate alternative, more balanced thoughts.

Cognitive Restructuring Strategies

- Operationalize the negative thought: a*sk for an example or definition* of a generalized statement.
- *Evaluate the utility,* implications, advantages, and disadvantages (the impact) of the thought or the belief.
- *Look at the accuracy* of the belief (Columns #4 and #5 of the Automatic Thought Record).
- Look at their thoughts like ideas that may not be true by *classifying thoughts as possible cognitive errors.*

David Burns's List of Cognitive Distortions

All or nothing (black/white)	Labeling
Jumping to conclusions	Catastrophizing
Magnification/minimization	Overgeneralizing
Disqualifying the positive	Mental filter
Should/must statements	Emotional reasoning
Mind reading	

(It's not important to identify exact cognitive errors in specific situations because many could apply.)

- *Help clients to see alternative ways around the situation* by thinking to themselves in a more productive way. Ask, *"What would you say to a friend in the same situation?"* Invite them to align how they treat others to how they would treat themselves (Column #6 of the thought record).
- Finally, have the clients *re-rate their moods* to see if there's any shift from the second column rating. An improvement will powerfully motivate clients to apply CBT on their own.

BEHAVIORAL ACTIVATION AND HOMEWORK

8. Homework helps clients to acquire skills, activate themselves, and problem solve.

One behavioral experiment is worth 100 Automatic Thought Records.

Have clients make specific predictions and then "test" those thoughts behaviorally. Changes occur through corrective experiences that disconfirm expectancies, not through cognitive restructuring alone.

- Start where the client really is, not where he or she expects to be.
- Collaboratively negotiate homework tasks that are relevant and feasible, with a rationale.
- Use activity scheduling. Be specific: what time of day, which specific days, what will be recorded (i.e., sense of mastery or pleasure), and how long is this task going to be going on for?

- Ask the client to record his or her sense of mastery and/or sense of pleasure.
- Divide larger tasks into small components that are easily achievable.
- Plan for difficulties and ways to overcome obstacles.

Appendix C: Answer Key

LESSON PLAN #1

A. Discussion

1. The information that goes into Column #1 of the thought record is the situation when a mood shift was noticed.

2. Two reasons the information in Column #1 should be as specific as possible:

   a. To pinpoint the moment when the change in emotion was noted

   b. To get the client as close to the situation, affect, and thoughts as possible

3. The information that goes into Column #2 of the thought record is a list of emotions the client is feeling along with ratings.

4. The intensity ratings are important to help clients become more aware of fluctuations in emotion and so that any changes in affect can be quantified.

5. Generally, suicidality is considered to be a thought, even though clients may report that they "feel" suicidal. In reality, they often feel sad or despondent, but they are thinking about suicide.

6. We cannot affect our emotions directly; thus if we feel suicidal, we're stuck. On the other hand, if we are thinking about suicide, perhaps there are other, more adaptive ways to think.

7. The "hot thought" is the thought that is most driving or associated with emotions.

8. Ways to empathically respond to distress or tearfulness during a session include, with a nonjudgmental, caring tone in your voice, *validating and reflecting* their distress or emotion, or asking them to further describe their feelings or thoughts in the present moment, which communicates your interest. When possible, use the clients' words to convey that you understand their experiences. For example, you might say something like, "I can see how upsetting this is as you describe what happened. You have every right to feel hurt when somebody treats you that way."

9. The following techniques can help a client identify a hot thought:
   a. The Downward Arrow Technique
   b. Asking him to visualize the situation and recall what he was thinking
   c. Socratic questioning
   d. Looking at the emotions as clues because they are related to thoughts

10. Many people avoid their thoughts or feelings, particularly if they are painful or distressing. Just being aware of your thoughts helps you to understand your emotions in some sort of context, rather than as random phenomena outside of your control.

11. Our early experiences and interactions help to define how we see the world. In CBT they shape our "core beliefs," which are fundamental ideas about how the world works. Core beliefs become activated and give rise to automatic thoughts in given situations. For example, a boy who was always told that he was stupid while growing up may have automatic thoughts related to his intelligence and capability in a wide variety of circumstances.

LESSON PLAN #2

A. Discussion

1. Evidence is objective and would be acceptable in a court of law. Thoughts are internal ideas that may or may not be accurate.

2. If the thought is ultimately going to be balanced and believable, we must make sure that we capture all objective evidence "for" and "against" the hot thought. The goal of CBT is to think realistically and in proportion to the situation, not just positively.

3. The balanced thought is a rewriting of the initial hot thought, but based entirely on the evidence generated in Columns #4 and #5.

4. Re-rating moods in the last column of the thought record is the affective payoff of the exercise. For clients to be motivated to continue to use this skill, they must have some objective proof that their moods can be affected by changing the way they think.

5. Two ways of modifying dysfunctional thoughts include the following:
   a. What you would say to a friend in a similar situation
   b. Operationalizing the thought
   c. Identifying the cognitive distortion

6. If there is no convincing evidence for or against a particular thought, you can use a "constructivist" approach. This approach dictates that since the situation is ambiguous and there is no convincing evidence in either direction, instead of looking at the accuracy of the thought, the client can look at the utility of the thought. This is done by constructing a two-column table that looks at the "advantages" and "disadvantages" of a particular way of thinking.

7. Clients have certain patterns of thinking that are internally consistent. It is much easier for them to identify evidence that supports their ways of thinking because those patterns have subtly accumulated over the course of years at the expense of the evidence against.

8. Two explanations for no mood change at the end of a thought record include the following:
   a. Evidence not fully gathered
   b. Picked the wrong hot thought
   c. Thought was already accurate

9. A client's hot thoughts are generated from underlying core beliefs or schemas that are consistent over time and manifest themselves in different situations. As a result, different situations may still

engender patterns of thought consistent with those underlying beliefs.

10. These beliefs are based on our early experiences and are generally formed by about the age of 6. In other words, we have a way of understanding the world from a very young age.

LESSON PLAN #3

A. Discussion

1. The following are common behavioral coping strategies employed by clients suffering from untreated depression:
   a. Tending to isolate themselves interpersonally
   b. Spending time at home or in bed
   c. Engaging in suicidal behaviors

2. Clients think negatively about themselves, the world, and the future when they are depressed. Given these negative cognitions, their patterns of interpersonal isolation and suicide make sense.

3. The following are two behavioral strategies designed to help clients with depression:
   a. Activity scheduling
   b. Activity ratings

4. Mastery is about a sense of accomplishment like doing the laundry, cleaning the dishes, or completing taxes, whereas pleasure is an activity that is enjoyable such as spending time with others, watching a movie, or eating ice cream.

5. For clients who do not feel able to accomplish a behavioral

task, the task should be broken down into small, manageable components. The mastery and pleasure ratings also serve as continued incentives.

6. That should be explicitly labeled as a thought. Thoughts in the cognitive model are not accepted as facts; rather, they are open to scrutiny and speculation. The client should be encouraged to test this thought.

7. You might encourage your client by emphasizing the physical and mental benefits of physical activity. You might ask them how they would have been spending their time if they had not gone on the walk. You may reassure them that part of the illness of depression is anhedonia (lack of pleasure) and that the goal of the task is not necessarily to feel pleasure immediately but to start to engage in more functional behaviors that might ultimately impact thoughts and feelings.

8. Clients can absolutely engage in behavioral tasks with friends or family. Interpersonal contact is an essential component of remitting depression.

9. This should be normalized as part of the illness of depression (low energy). Clients should be reminded that they are ill and that it may take some time to regain their stamina. Thoughts around this decreased level of function may also be explored.

10. The fact that clients can still feel pleasure despite their illness should be emphasized. Similar activities should be scheduled into the following week on the activity log at an increased frequency. Clients can reflect on how their thoughts or predictions about the value of the activities were not totally

accurate, which may provide an incentive to have them try other activities they may not predict as pleasurable or useful.

LESSON PLAN #4

A. Discussion

Case #1

1. Cognitive distortions employed by Claire include the following:
   a. Catastrophization
   b. Labeling
   c. Future telling
   d. Emotional reasoning
2. Evidence to counter dysfunctional beliefs includes the following:
   a. The children are thriving
   b. She does well with children at school
   c. The children are in an excellent daycare
   d. The children are only at daycare 8 hours during the day
   e. This is a common scenario and most children do fine
3. CBT probably will not make her feel 100% okay about her kids being in daycare. While she has clear cognitive distortions, she is spending a portion of the day away from them. However, CBT may help with her fears about the impact of daycare.
4. Claire may realize she meets many of her own criteria for being a "good mother." Further, it gives her specific behavioral targets in the areas in which she falls short.
5. You might point out that other parents leave their children with her. You might highlight her skills with children. You might ask

her to reflect on how her pupils deal with time away from their parents.

Case #2

1. Cognitions behind Bob's interpersonal isolation include the following:
   a. I'm useless
   b. I'll bring people down
   c. What's the point?
2. Get Bob to commit to a specific trip to the grocery store. Have him rate his mood on the day when he prepares his own food versus a day when he eats from a can. If necessary, break the task down into small components and problem solve in advance around obstacles.
3. Try to identify the cognitions associated with the noncompliance, such as "it won't work" or "I can't do it." Make sure the homework task was clear. Make the tasks easier if necessary.
4. One should never adopt the stance of trying to convince a client of a particular course of action in CBT. However, you may do some activity scheduling to allow him to come to the realization that his moods are often worse when he lies in bed. You may also have him try out different behaviors to see if they result in different mood states.
5. Bob would be helped by performing any behavior that results in a sense of mastery or pleasure. Also, he could do any activity that involves improved health and self-care or that allows for interpersonal contact.

QUIZ

1. List at least five key principles or characteristics of cognitive therapy treatment. (Correct answers can include any of the following.)

    - The cognitive triad that links automatic thoughts, feelings, and behaviors
    - Use of the Automatic Thought Record
    - Socratic questioning, or guided discovery, that include operationalizing a negative thought (with a definition or example); evaluating the utility and impact of the thought; looking at the accuracy of the belief by examining the evidence for and against it; using the Burns's list of cognitive distortions; and helping them to see an alternative view
    - Behavioral activation and the use of homework, such as activity scheduling
    - Look for patterns of beliefs in the domains of lovability or achievement
    - Use the Downward Arrow Technique to identify core beliefs

2. b. Automatic thoughts
3. b. Examining the evidence
4. d. Private
5. c. Reacting with sadness
6. a. Unconscious thoughts
7. c. A, C, and D
8. d. Labeling cognitive errors or distortions

9. a. Listing advantages and disadvantages
10. b. Use an activity schedule, recording levels of mastery and pleasure
11. c. They are upsetting emotions.
12. d. CBT focuses on relationships and the unconscious.
13. a. People have more control over their feelings than their thoughts and behaviors.
14. b. Some are genetic
15. c. The Automatic Thought Record
16. b. Asking friends and family to remind you to cheer up
17. a. Core beliefs cause stressful events
18. b. It can work effectively only if the client completes all seven columns
19. c. That the homework will be viewed as successful if she experiences a decrease in symptoms as a result
20. a. Asking the client to do the opposite of her negative thought
21. c. Behavioral symptoms, such as avoiding contact with friends or family
22. d. All of the above
23. a. A and C
24. d. In stirring strong negative emotions, it weakens the therapeutic alliance.
25. a. Changing the views that people take of things

References

Beck, A. T. (2005). The current state of cognitive therapy: A 40-year retrospective. *Archives of General Psychiatry, 62*(9), 953–959.

Beck, A. T., & Hurvich, M. S. (1959). Psychological correlates of depression: Frequency of "masochistic" dream content in a private practice sample. *Psychosomatic Medicine, 21*(1), 50–55.

Beck, A. T., Rush, A. J., Shaw, B. F., & Emery, G. (1979). *Cognitive therapy of depression.* New York, NY: Guilford Press.

Burns, D. (1999). *The feeling good handbook: The new mood therapy.* New York, NY: Plume.

Epictetus. (2008). *Discourses and selected writings* (trans. and ed. Robert Dobbin). New York, NY: Penguin Classics.

Greenberger D., & Padesky, C. A. (1995). *Mind over mood: Changing the way you feel by changing the way you think.* New York, NY: Guilford Press.

Lambert, M. J., & Barley, D. E. (2001). Research summary on the therapeutic relationship and psychotherapy outcome. *Psychotherapy, 38*(4), 357–361.

Ravitz, P., Cooke, R.G., Mitchell, S., Reeves, S., Teshima, J., Lokuge, B., . . . Zaretsky, A. (2013). Continuing education to go: Capacity building in psychotherapies for front-line mental health workers in underserviced communities. *Canadian Journal of Psychiatry, 58* (6).

Rogers, C. R. (1957). The necessary and sufficient conditions of therapeutic personality change. *Journal of Consulting Psychology, 21,* 95–103.

Rogers, C. R. (1961). *On becoming a person: A therapist's view of psychotherapy.* New York, NY: Houghton Mifflin.